CANADIAN CORRECTIONS OFFICER TEST PREP

CSC Correctional Officer Study
Guide with Practice Questions

Copyright © 2024 by Complete Test Preparation Inc. ALL RIGHTS RESERVED.

No part of this book may be reproduced or transferred in any form or by any means, graphic, electronic, or mechanical, including photocopying, recording, web distribution, taping, or by any information storage retrieval system, without the written permission of the author.

Notice: Complete Test Preparation Inc. makes every reasonable effort to obtain from reliable sources accurate, complete, and timely information about the tests covered in this book. Nevertheless, changes can be made in the tests or the administration of the tests at any time and Complete Test Preparation Inc. makes no representation or warranty, either expressed or implied as to the accuracy, timeliness, or completeness of the information contained in this book. Complete Test Preparation Inc. make no representations or warranties of any kind, express or implied, about the completeness, accuracy, reliability, suitability or availability with respect to the information contained in this document for any purpose. Any reliance you place on such information is therefore strictly at your own risk.

The author(s) shall not be liable for any loss incurred as a consequence of the use and application, directly or indirectly, of any information presented in this work. Sold with the understanding, the author is not engaged in rendering professional services or advice. If advice or expert assistance is required, the services of a competent professional should be sought.

The company, product and service names used in this publication are for identification purposes only. All trademarks and registered trademarks are the property of their respective owners. Complete Test Preparation Inc. is not affiliated with any educational institution or the Federal government.

Complete Test Preparation Inc. is not affiliated with, or endorsed by Correctional Service of Canada. All organizational and test names are trademarks of their respective owners.

We strongly recommend that students check with exam providers for up-to-date information regarding test content.

Please note that the Corrections Officer test is administered by Correctional Service of Canada, which was not involved in the production of, and does not endorse, this product.

All material presented here is for SKILL PRACTICE ONLY.

Version 8.5 July 2024

ISBN: 9781772454352

About Complete Test Preparation Inc.

Why Us?
The Complete Test Preparation Team has been publishing high quality study materials since 2005, with a catalogue of over 145 titles, in English, French, Spanish and Chinese, as well as ESL curriculum for all levels.

To keep up with the industry changes, we update everything all the time!

And the best part?
With every purchase, you're helping people all over the world improve themselves and their education. So thank you in advance for supporting this mission with us! Together, we are truly making a difference in the lives of those often forgotten by the system.

Charities that we support
https://www.test-preparation.ca/charities-and-non-profits/
You have definitely come to the right place.
If you want to spend your valuable study time where it will help you the most - we've got you covered today and tomorrow.

https://www.test-preparation.ca

FEEDBACK

We welcome your feedback. Email us at feedback@test-preparation.ca with your comments and suggestions. We carefully review all suggestions and often incorporate reader suggestions into upcoming versions. As a Print on Demand Publisher, we update our products frequently.

https://www.facebook.com/CompleteTestPreparation/

https://www.youtube.com/user/MrTestPreparation

Contents

8 Getting Started
　　How this study guide is organized　9
　　The Corrections Officer Test Study Plan　9
　　Making a Study Schedule　10

15 WCPT
　　Ordering Sentences, Reading and
　　Sentence Correction Self Assessment　18
　　Answer Key　36
　　Vocabulary Self Assessment　38
　　Answer Key　46
　　Help with Reading Comprehension　48
　　Main Idea and Supporting Details　51
　　Help with Building your Vocabulary　55

59 English Grammar and Usage
　　Practice questions　60
　　Answer Key　68
　　English Grammar & Punctuation Tutorials　71
　　Capitalization　71
　　Punctuation　73
　　Hyphens　74
　　Apostrophes　76
　　Commas　77
　　Quotation Marks　79
　　Subject Verb Agreement　81

88 Practice Test Questions Set 1
　　Answer Key　136

152 Practice Test Questions Set 2
　　Answer Key　197

213 Conclusion

GETTING STARTED

CONGRATULATIONS! By deciding to take the CSC Corrections Officer Test, you have taken the first step toward a great future! Of course, there is no point in taking this important examination unless you intend to do your best to earn the highest grade you possibly can. That means getting yourself organized and discovering the best approaches, methods and strategies to master the material. Yes, that will require real effort and dedication on your part, but if you are willing to focus your energy and devote the study time necessary, before you know it you will be on you way to a brighter future.

We know that taking on a new endeavour can be scary, and it is easy to feel unsure of where to begin. That's where we come in. This study guide is designed to help you improve your test-taking skills, show you a few tricks of the trade and increase both your competency and confidence.

The CSC Corrections Officer Test

The Corrections Officer Test has three modules, English Language Arts and Math. The English Language Arts consists of English grammar and usage, vocabulary and an essay. The Math module contains basic High School math.

While we seek to make our guide as comprehensive as possible, note that like all entrance exams, the Corrections Officer Test might be adjusted at some future point. New material might be added, or content that is no longer relevant or applicable might be removed. It is always a good idea to give the materials you receive when you register to take the Test a careful review.

Getting Started

How this study guide is organized

This study guide is divided into three sections. The first section, Self-Assessments, which will help you recognize your areas of strength and weaknesses. This will be a boon when it comes to managing your study time most efficiently; there is not much point of focusing on material you have already got firmly under control. Instead, taking the self-assessments will show you where that time could be much better spent. In this area you will begin with a few questions to evaluate quickly your understanding of material that is likely to appear on the Corrections Officer Test. If you do poorly in certain areas, simply work carefully through those sections in the tutorials and then try the self-assessment again.

The second section, Tutorials, offers information in each of the content areas, as well as strategies to help you master that material. The tutorials are not intended to be a complete course, but cover general principles. If you find that you do not understand the tutorials, it is recommended that you seek out additional instruction.

Third, we offer two sets of practice test questions, similar to those on the test. Again, we cover all modules, so make sure to check with your school!

The Corrections Officer Test Study Plan

Now that you have made the decision to take the test, it is time to get started. Before you do another thing, you will need to figure out a plan of attack. The best study tip is to start early! The longer the time period you devote to regular study practice, the likelier that you will retain the material and access it quickly. If you thought that 1 x 20 is the same as 2 x 10, guess what? It really is not, when it comes to study time. Reviewing material for just an hour per day over the course of 20 days is far better than studying for two hours a day for only 10 days. The more often you revisit a particular piece of information, the better you will know it. Not only will your grasp and understanding be better, but your ability to reach into your brain and quickly and efficiently pull out the tidbit you need, will be greatly enhanced as well.

The great Chinese scholar and philosopher Confucius believed that true knowledge could be defined as knowing what you know and what you do not know. The first step in preparing for the test is to assess your strengths and weaknesses. You may already have an idea of what you know and what you do not know, but evaluating yourself using our Self- Assessment modules for each of the three areas, Math, English and Reading Comprehension, will clarify the details.

Making a Study Schedule

To make your study time the most productive, you will need to develop a study plan. The purpose of the plan is to organize all the bits of pieces of information in such a way that you will not feel overwhelmed. Rome was not built in a day, and learning everything you will need to know to pass the Corrections Officer Test is going to take time, too. Arranging the material you need to learn into manageable chunks is the best way to go. Each study session should make you feel as though you have accomplished your goal, or at least are a little closer, and your goal is simply to learn what you planned to learn during that particular session. Try to organize the content in such a way that each study session builds on previous ones. That way, you will retain the information, be better able to access it, and review the previous bits and pieces at the same time.

GETTING STARTED

Self-assessment

The Best Study Tip! The best study tip is to start early! The longer you study regularly, the more you will retain and 'learn' the material. Studying for 1 hour per day for 20 days is far better than studying for 2 hours for 10 days.

What don't you know?

The first step is to assess your strengths and weaknesses. You may already have an idea of where your weaknesses are, or you can take our Self-assessment modules for each of the areas, WCPT and Situational Judgement.

Exam Component	Rate from 1 to 5
English / Language Arts	
Vocabulary	
Grammar & Usage	
Punctuation	
Capitalization	
Main Idea	
Reading	
Summarizing	
Situational Judgement	

Making a Study Schedule

The key to a successful study plan is to divide the material you need to learn into manageable size and learn it, while at the same time reviewing the material that you already know.

Using the table above, any scores of three or below, mean you need to spend time learning, reviewing and practicing this subject area. A score of four means you need to review the material, but you don't have to spend time re-learning. A score of five and you are OK with just an occasional review

before the exam.
A score of zero or one means you really do need to work on this and you should allocate the most time and give it the highest priority. Some students prefer a 5-day plan and others a 10-day plan. It also depends on how much time you have until the exam.

Here is an example of a 5-day plan based on an example from the table above:

Punctuation: 1   Study 1 hour everyday – review on last day
Main Idea: 3   Study 1 hour for 2 days then ½ hour and then review
Vocabulary: 4   Review every second day
Grammar & Usage: 2 Study 1 hour on the first day – then ½ hour everyday
Reading Comprehension: 5   Review for ½ hour every other day
Situational Judgement: 5 Review for ½ hour every other day

Using this example, Situational Judgement and reading comprehension are good and only need occasional review. Vocabulary is good and needs 'some' review. Main Idea need a bit of work, grammar and usage needs a lot of work and Punctuation is very weak and need most time. Based on this, here is a sample study plan:

Day	Subject	Time
Monday		
Study	Punctuation	1 hour
Study	Grammar & Usage	1 hour
	½ hour break	
Study	Main Idea	1 hour
Review	Vocabulary	½ hour
Tuesday		
Study	Punctuation	1 hour

GETTING STARTED

Study	Grammar & Usage	½ hour
	½ hour break	
Study	Main Idea	½ hour
Review	Vocabulary	½ hour
Review	Situational Judgement	½ hour
Wednesday		
Study	Punctuation	1 hour
Study	Grammar & Usage	½ hour
	½ hour break	
Study	Main Idea	½ hour
Review	Situational Judgement	½ hour
Thursday		
Study	Punctuation	½ hour
Study	Grammar & Usage	½ hour
Review	Main Idea	½ hour
	½ hour break	
Review	Situational Judgement	½ hour
Review	Vocabulary	½ hour
Friday		
Review	Punctuation	½ hour
Review	Grammar & Usage	½ hour
Review	Main Idea	½ hour
	½ hour break	
Review	Vocabulary	½ hour
Review	Grammar & Usage	½ hour

Using this example, adapt the study plan to your own schedule. This schedule assumes 2 ½ - 3 hours available to study everyday for a 5 day period.

First, write out what you need to study and how much. Next figure out how many days you have before the test. Note, do NOT study on the last day before the test. On the last day before the test, you won't learn anything and will probably only confuse yourself.

Make a table with the days before the test and the number of hours you have available to study each day. We suggest working with 1 hour and ½ hour time slots.

Start filling in the blanks, with the subjects you need to study the most getting the most time and the most regular time slots (i.e. everyday) and the subjects that you know getting the least time (e.g. ½ hour every other day, or every 3rd day).

Tips for making a schedule

Once you make a schedule, stick with it! Make your study sessions reasonable. If you make a study schedule and don't stick with it, you set yourself up for failure. Instead, schedule study sessions that are a bit shorter and set yourself up for success! Make sure your study sessions are do-able. Studying is hard work but after you pass, you can party and take a break!

Schedule breaks. Breaks are just as important as study time. Work out a rotation of studying and breaks that works for you.

Build up study time. If you find it hard to sit still and study for 1 hour straight through, build up to it. Start with 20 minutes, and then take a break. Once you get used to 20-minute study sessions, increase the time to 30 minutes. Gradually work you way up to 1 hour.

40 minutes to 1 hour is optimal. Studying for longer than this is tiring and not productive. Studying for shorter isn't long enough to be productive.

Studying Math. Studying Math is different from studying other subjects because you use a different part of your brain. The best way to study math is to practice everyday. This will train your mind to think in a mathematical way. If you miss a day or days, the mathematical mind-set is gone and you have to start all over again to build it up.

Study and practice math everyday for at least 5 days before the exam.

WCPT

THIS SECTION CONTAINS A SELF-ASSESSMENT AND TUTORIALS. The tutorials are designed to familiarize general principles and the self-assessment contains general questions similar to the questions likely to be on the Corrections Officer Test, but are not intended to be identical to the exam questions. The tutorials are not designed to be a complete course, and it is assumed that students have some familiarity with these questions. If you do not understand parts of the tutorial, or find the tutorial difficult, it is recommended that you seek out additional instruction.

Note that these questions are for skill practice only.

Tour of the WCPT Content

Below is a detailed list of the types of questions that generally appear on the test.

- Identifying grammar mistakes
- Choosing the best title for a passage
- Sentence and paragraph order

- Summarizing
- Punctuation
- Vocabulary
- English usage
- Avoiding wordiness and redundancy
- Main idea and details

The questions below are not the same as you will find on the WCPT - that would be too easy! And nobody knows what the questions will be and they change all the time. Mostly the changes consist of substituting new questions for old, but the changes can be new question formats or styles, changes to the number of questions in each section, changes to the time limits for each section and combining sections. Below are general reading questions that cover the same areas as the WCPT. So, while the format and exact wording of the questions may differ slightly, and change from year to year, if you can answer the questions below, you will have no problem with the reading section of the WCPT.

WCPT Self-Assessment

The purpose of the self-assessment is:

- Identify your strengths and weaknesses.
- Develop your personalized study plan (above)
- Get accustomed to the WCPT format
- Extra practice – the self-assessments are almost a full 3rd practice test!
- Provide a baseline score for preparing your study schedule.

Since this is a Self-assessment, and depending on how

confident you are with Reading Comprehension, timing is optional. The WCPT has 35 reading questions. The self-assessment has 12 questions, so allow about 15 minutes to complete this assessment.

Once complete, use the table below to assess your understanding of the content, and prepare your study schedule described in chapter 1.

80% - 100%	Excellent – you have mastered the content
60 – 79%	Good. You have a working knowledge. Even though you can just pass this section, you may want to review the Tutorials and do some extra practice to see if you can improve your mark.
40% - 59%	Below Average. You do not understand the reading comprehension problems. Review the tutorials, and retake this quiz again in a few days, before proceeding to the rest of the Practice Test Questions.
Less than 40%	Poor. You have a very limited understanding of the reading comprehension problems. Please review the Tutorials, and retake this quiz again in a few days, before proceeding to the Practice Test Questions.

ORDERING SENTENCES

```
    A B C D
 1  ○ ○ ○ ○
 2  ○ ○ ○ ○
 3  ○ ○ ○ ○
 4  ○ ○ ○ ○
 5  ○ ○ ○ ○
 6  ○ ○ ○ ○
 7  ○ ○ ○ ○
 8  ○ ○ ○ ○
 9  ○ ○ ○ ○
10  ○ ○ ○ ○
```

WCPT Self Assessment

READING, AND SENTENCE CORRECTION

	A	B	C	D
1	○	○	○	○
2	○	○	○	○
3	○	○	○	○
4	○	○	○	○
5	○	○	○	○
6	○	○	○	○
7	○	○	○	○
8	○	○	○	○
9	○	○	○	○
10	○	○	○	○

Instructions Questions 1 - 5: The first sentence of a paragraph is given below, followed by additional sentences in the paragraph, listed in no particular order. Order the sentences to create the best paragraph. Make sure the paragraph is properly organized and grammatically correct.

1.

A. With so much information available, employers are looking for data scientists to help sort, clean, analyze, process and manage it for them.
B. More precisely, in 2020, there were around 44 zettabytes of data in the world.
C. Nearly every organization today is sitting on massive amounts of data.
D. Also known as 'Big Data', this information is being collected every day by businesses all over the world.

    a. ACDB
    b. DCBA
    c. CBAD
    d. CDBA

2.

A. Instead, The Tempest relegates the homecoming of Prospero to offstage action after the epilogue, which further blurs the line between theatre and reality.
B. To emphasize duality, The Tempest possesses a peculiarity in its treatment of clothing: Prospero removes or changes his costume at key moments in the first and final acts.
C. In effect, the play postpones one drama and begins another.
D. William Shakespeare's The Tempest focuses on Prospero's return to Milan yet withholds the pleasure of a complete homecoming for its protagonist.

    a. ABCD
    b. BDAC
    c. DBAC
    d. DABC

3.

A. In a globalized and secularized society with technological advancements that never slow down, "Religion" proper appears to have lost efficacy due to its rhetorical association with an arcane and unfamiliar past.
B. The limiting nature of such literary-religious conversations and the normative force it carries can be attributed to a much broader trend in the academic world and beyond, namely secularization.
C. Religious conversations in literary studies tend to be limiting in that religion often becomes mythologized as a modality of the past, and this creates a dynamic in literary criticism where religion is considered worthy as a symbolic anchor within a text but is not given due consideration as a contemporary social issue.
D. The intentionality behind this phenomenon is hardly overt, and instead it arises as a specter of an unspoken agreement.

    a. ACDB
    b. CDBA
    c. CBDA
    d. ABCD

4.
A. If not providing a clear answer, then Ariel, at the very least, tracks the complexity and even impossibility of any single solution.
B. Sylvia Plath's posthumously published poetry collection, Ariel, is perhaps best defined by the vivid imagery that delves deep into Plath's psyche.
C. Time and time again, Ariel seems to return to essential questions about Plath's identity.
D. Throughout the collection, Plath explores dimensions of herself: her past, present, and future.

    a. DBCA
    b. BDCA
    c. CDAB
    d. BCDA

5.
A. Other countries have their own versions of Santa Claus.
B. However, that is just one depiction of the generous being that brings toys to well-behaved children on Christmas Eve.
C. Santa Claus is a jolly, white-haired man in a red suit for most Americans.
D. Who, in some cases, do not even appear during Christmas.

   a. CADB
   b. ADCB
   c. CDBA
   d. CBAD

6.
A. But it also helped change Victorian society as it boosted people's awareness of the plight of the poor in Victorian England.
B. A Christmas Carol was published in 1843, and it ensured that Charles Dickens' name would forever be linked with Christmas.
C. It includes extremes such as wealth and poverty, industry, and inability.
D. This gives it a feel of a very Victorian story of urban circumstances.

   a. BABD
   b. DABC
   c. BDAC
   d. BCDA

7.

A. That's based on population trends and ongoing waste management disposal problems, although there may be some early signs of change.
B. And if the biggest polluters don't clean up how they throw stuff away, by 2025, the total accumulated plastic trash in the oceans will reach around 170 million tons.
C. Each year, about 8.8 million tons of plastic end up in the world's oceans.
D. That's the equivalent of five grocery bags full of plastic debris dotting each foot of coastline around the world.

   a. CDAB
   b. CABD
   c. CDBA
   d. CBAD

8.

A. Smartphones and game controllers offer haptic feedback to users through vibrations.
B. The word haptic is used to describe things related to the sense of touch.
C. Future haptic devices could also use sound waves we can't hear to make users feel objects that aren't there.
D. The skin is full of receptors that send different types of haptic information — such as texture or pressure — to the brain.

   a. CABD
   b. BDAC
   c. BCAD
   d. DBAC

9.
A. The placebo used in such medical works is usually a pill that looks the same as the treatment but contains no medicine.
B. A person may feel better after taking a placebo pill at times, even though the tablet did not act on any disease or symptoms.
C. They are used to prove that a new medicine works; researchers must show that people taking it heal more than people getting a placebo.
D. Placebos are an essential part of medical research.

    a. DACB
    b. DBCA
    c. ADCB
    d. DCAB

0.
A. It functions as an insecticide in plants — poisoning insects that try to eat the plant.
B. That makes it harder and harder to stop using it.
C. Humans, however, get very different effects from nicotine - It stimulates them and relaxes them too.
D. Nicotine is an addictive substance found primarily on tobacco plants.
E. Unfortunately, nicotine is highly addictive, so the more someone uses it, the more they crave its effects.

    a. DEACB
    b. DAECB
    c. DACEB
    d. DCEBA

Reading

Question 1 refers to the following passage.

Was Dr. Seuss a Real Doctor?

A favorite author for over 100 years, Theodor Seuss Geisel was born on March 2, 1902. Today, we celebrate the birthday of the famous "Dr. Seuss" by hosting Read Across America events throughout the March. School children around the country celebrate the "Doctor's" birthday by making hats, giving presentations and holding read aloud circles featuring some of Dr. Seuss' most famous books.

But who was Dr. Seuss? Did he go to medical school? Where was his office? You may be surprised to know that Theodor Seuss Geisel was not a medical doctor at all. He took on the nickname Dr. Seuss when he became a noted children's book author. He earned the nickname because people said his books were "as good as medicine." All these years later, his nickname has lasted and he is known as Dr. Seuss all across the world.

Think back to when you were a young child. Did you ever want to try "green eggs and ham?" Did you try to "Hop on Pop?" Do you remember learning about the environment from a creature called The Lorax? Of course, you must recall one of Seuss' most famous characters; that green Grinch who stole Christmas. These stories were all written by Dr. Seuss and featured his signature rhyming words and letters. They also featured made up words to enhance his rhyme scheme and even though many of his characters were made up, they sure seem real to us today.

And what of his "signature" book, The Cat in the Hat? You must remember that cat and Thing One and Thing Two from your childhood. Did you know that in the early 1950's there was a growing concern in America that children were not becoming avid readers? This was, book publishers thought, because children found books dull and uninteresting. An intelligent publisher sent Dr. Seuss a book of words that he thought all children should learn as young readers. Dr. Seuss wrote his famous story The Cat in the Hat, using those words. We can see, over the decades, just how much influence his writing has had on very young children. That is why we celebrate this doctor's birthday each March.

1. The theme of this passage is

    a. Dr. Seuss was not a doctor.

    b. Dr. Seuss influenced the lives of generations of young children.

    c. Dr. Seuss wrote rhyming books.

    d. Dr. Seuss' birthday is a good day to read a book.

Question 2 refers to the following passage.

The Civil War

The Civil War began on April 12, 1861. The first shots of the Civil War were fired in Fort Sumter, South Carolina. Note that even though more American lives were lost in the Civil War than in any other war, not one person died on that first day. The war began because eleven Southern states seceded from the Union and tried to start their own government, The Confederate States of America.

Why did the states secede? The issue of slavery was a primary cause of the Civil War. The eleven southern states relied heavily on their slaves to foster their farming and plantation lifestyles. The northern states, many of whom had already abolished slavery, did not feel that the southern states should have slaves. The north wanted to free all the slaves and President Lincoln's goal was to both end slavery and preserve the Union. He had Congress declare war on the Confederacy on April 14, 1862. For four long, blood soaked years, the North and South fought.

From 1861 to mid 1863, it seemed as if the South would win this war. However, on July 1, 1863, an epic three day battle was waged on a field in Gettysburg, Pennsylvania. Gettysburg is remembered for being the bloodiest battle in American history. At the end of the three days, the North turned the tide of the war in their favour.

The North then went on to dominate the South for the remainder of the war. A famous episode is General Sherman's "March to The Sea," where he famously led the Union Army through Georgia and the Carolinas, burning and destroying everything in their path.

In 1865, the Union army invaded and captured the Confederate capital of Richmond Virginia. Robert E. Lee, leader of the Confederacy surrendered to General Ulysses S. Grant, leader of the Union forces, on April 9, 1865. The Civil War was over and the Union was preserved.

2. Which of the following statements summarizes a FACT from the passage?

 a. Congress declared war and then the Battle of Fort Sumter began.

 b. Congress declared war after shots were fired at Fort Sumter.

 c. President Lincoln was pro slavery

 d. President Lincoln was at Fort Sumter with Congress

Questions 3 refers to the following passage.

Hansel and Gretel

. . . The boy was called Hansel and the girl Gretel. He had little to bite and to break, and once when great dearth fell on the land, he could no longer procure even daily bread. Now when he thought over this by night in his bed, and tossed about in his anxiety, he groaned and said to his wife: 'What is to become of us? How are we to feed our poor children, when we no longer have anything even for ourselves?' 'I'll tell you what, husband,' answered the woman, 'early tomorrow morning we will take the children out into the forest to where it is the thickest; there we will light a fire for them, and give each of them one more piece of bread, and then we will go to our work and leave them alone. They will not find the way home again, and we shall be rid of them.' 'No, wife,' said the man, 'I will not do that; how can I bear to leave my children alone in the forest?—the wild animals would soon come and tear them to pieces.' 'O, you fool!' said she, 'then we must all four die of hunger, you may as well plane the planks for our coffins,' and she left him no peace until he consented . . . .

from *Hansel and Gretel by Jacob and Wilhelm Grimm*

3. Which of the following is the best topic sentence for the passage?

    a. There once was a rich man who dwelt in a great forest with his wife and his two children.

    b. Close to a great forest dwelt a poor wood-cutter with his wife and his two children.

    c. Once upon a time, deep in the forest, dwelt a happy, loving family with two children.

    d. The Black Forest was home to a king and his two children, a boy and a girl.

Question 4 refers to the following passage.

Boys on an Island

. . . Then they cooked some bacon in the frying pan and used up half of their corn bread. It was glorious to feast on an unexplored, uninhabited island. The boys agreed that they never would return to civilization. The fire lit their faces and threw its reddish glare on tree trunks and vines . . . .

from *The Adventures of Tom Sawyer by Mark Twain*

4. Which of the following is the best first sentence for the passage?

a. Tom had procured some bacon from his aunt to be used as sustenance for the day's adventure.

b. Tom and Huck avoided school that morning and went into town for supplies.

c. They built a fire alongside a large log about twenty steps inside the forest.

d. They had always enjoyed paddling down river looking for campsites.

Sentence Correction

A Personal Satellite?

Questions 5 - 8 refer to the following passage

Many of us are already so loaded with technology, we don't have time to think about integrating even more! [1] In fact at this point it seems impossible to think about personal satellites now, just as we once thought about smart phones. [2] The reality of personal spacecraft is still in the realm of Star Trek and geeky space fantasies. [3]

However, the days when each of us will have our own personal satellite are not far away! [4] And what is even more exciting is they will be available for the cost of an iPhone! [5] At least, according to Zach Manchester, the inventor of the nano-satellite KickSat. [6] "I'd like to think of it as the people's satellite," says Manchester. [7] "We're pushing towards a personal satellite, where you can afford to put your own thing in space." [8]

The KickSat, a 30 cm. long hardware pack, is a space enthusiast's dream. [9] It contains the basics of a fully functional satellite. [10] Inside its compact design, the KickSat itself contains 200 more tinier satellites of cubic shape called

"Sprites." [11] The Sprites are engineered and programmed so that they can be tracked and communicate via radio signals with a ground station on earth. [12] Each Sprite is available for purchase and is uniquely named after the sponsors who support Zach's project. [13] Anyone who has sponsored a Sprite will be able to track their personal satellite from a ground station installed in their balcony or roof! [14]

5. Which sentence from the passage is an example of a sentence fragment?

    a. 4
    b. 7
    c. 6
    d. 10

6. Which of the following sentences should be edited to reduce redundancy?

    a. 5
    b. 4
    c. 10
    d. 16

7. Which of the following changes are needed to sentence 2?

    a. In fact at this point it seems impossible to think about personal satellites now - just as we once thought about smart phones.

    b. In fact, at this point, it seems impossible to think about personal satellites now, just as we once thought about smart phones.

    c. In fact, at this point, it seems impossible to think about personal satellites now - just as we once thought about smart phones.

    d. In fact at this point, it seems impossible to think about personal satellites now, just as we once thought about smart phones.

8. Which of the following changes are needed to sentence 11?

a. Under its compact design, the KickSat itself contains 200 more tiny satellites of cubic shape called "Sprites."

b. Under its compact design, the KickSat itself contains 200 more tiny satellites of cubic shapes called "Sprites."

c. Inside its compact design, the KickSat itself contains 200 tinier satellites of cubic shapes called "Sprites."

d. With its compact design, the KickSat contains 200 tiny cube-shaped satellites called "Sprites."

Alvin Lee's Guitar

Questions 9 and 10 refer to the following passage

Only a few of his contemporaries rocked the rock n' roll era with their guitars like Alvin Lee. [1] Even at the age of 67, just a year before his demise, he produced one of the finest albums of his five-decade long career with *Still on the Road to Freedom*. [2] Strikingly flamboyant with his guitar, Lee gained millions of admirers around the world with hits like *"I'd Love to Change the World," "On the Road to Freedom"* and *"Freedom for the Stallion"* which reflected popular worldviews at the time of their release. [3]

Alvin Lee began playing guitar at an early age, and was influenced by his parents' passion for music and inspired by the likes of Chuck Berry and Scotty Moore. [4] Lee started his career as the lead vocalist and guitarist in a band named the Jaybirds at the famous Marquee Club in London in 1962. [5] A few years later the band changed its name to *Ten Years After* and released its debut album under the new name. [6] Lee's lightning fast guitar playing at the Woodstock Festival gained him instant stardom and Lee was asked to tour the US. [7]

In the coming years, he worked with rock legends like Mylon LeFevre, George Harrison, Steve Winwood, Ronnie Wood and Mick Fleetwood and released the country rock masterpiece *On the Road to Freedom* which brought him overwhelming trans-Atlantic popularity. [8] In subsequent years, he continued addressing social and global issues in albums like *A Space in Time*, *Pump Iron!*, *Let It Rock* and *Rocket Fuel*. [9] With many of his songs, such as, "I'd Love to Change the World," Lee used the power of rock music to show his solidarity with ordinary people and their worldviews. [10] He also went on with inspiring the upcoming generations of rock stars by producing expressive and tasteful guitar performances in his 1980s albums *Free Fall*, *RX5* and *Detroit Diesel*. [11]

9. Which sentence in the second paragraph is the least relevant to the main idea of the second paragraph?

    a. 4

    b. 5

    c. 6

    d. 7

10. Which of the following sentences, if inserted before sentence 11, would best illustrate the main idea of the passage?

    a. His charismatic personality earned him more fame and led him to perform even better for the sake of his admirers.

    b. As he gained popularity because of his artistic creations he tried to implant political motives into his music.

    c. At the same time, he thought of doing something for the future generations.

    d. With the creative songs he composed, he established himself as an exemplary figure among fellow guitarists and the generations that followed.

Answer Key

Sentence Order

1. C

The opening sentence is C as it introduces the topic, and all the other sentences contain transitional words. Then comes B, which specifies the amount of the information. The next sentence is D that gives a name to this huge amount of data and lastly, A notes that due to this companies are looking for data scientists.

2. D

The first sentence is D as it presents the topic. Then comes A as it explains the meaning of the previous information. The following one is B as it refers to the duality expressed prior. The last one left is C.

3. B

The first sentence can be either C or However, as all the other sentences are about religious motifs in literature, the opening sentence should set the topic for that. Additionally, A is clearly a follow-up to B as it explains the role of secularization in the phenomenon. Thus, the first sentence will be C, followed by D as 'this phenomenon" refers to sentence C. The following ones are B and A.

4. B

The opening sentence is B, as all the others contain transitional words. Then comes D, as it gives additional details about Plath's poetry collection. C and A form one thought at the end.

5. D

The first sentence is C, as all the others contain transitional words. The following sentence contradicts this one with the connecting word - 'however'. A and D form one thought to create the contradictory information mentioned in sentence B.

6. D

The first sentence is B as it introduces the topic, and all the others contain transitional words. D and A form one thought as D is in contrast with A that although the story is very Victorian, it changed the Victorian society as well. So the second sentence will be C which describes the book, and the last two D followed by A.

7. C

The opening sentence is C as all the others contain transitional words suggesting that there was some information provided prior. The second sentence is D, as it gives a comparison to understand the situation of the world's ocean. The third one will be B, which shows the threat we might face if the pollution continues, and A, which gives hope.

8. B

The opening sentence is B as it introduces a new term - haptic. Then comes D, which continues the thought. The following is A adding different information and C as it contains future possibilities.

9. D

The first sentence should be D as it presents the new topic. Sentence A is the follow-up to C as 'such medical work' refers to the information in C. B is the follow-up to A as it mentioned placebo pill. So the correct order is D, then C, A, and lastly B.

10. C

The opening sentence is D as it presents the general topic -Nicotine. Then comes A as it gives the details on what the nicotine does for the plants. The following sentence is C as it contains the connective word - 'However' and suggests a contrasting thought that Nicotine works differently in humans. B is a follow-up to E as the transitional word 'That' refers to addictiveness mentioned in E.

WCPT Self Assessment

Reading and Usage

1. B
The passage describes in detail how Dr. Seuss had a great effect on the lives of children through his writing. It names several of his books, tells how he helped children become avid readers and explains his style of writing.

Choice A is incorrect because that is just one single fact about the passage. Choice C is incorrect because that is just one single fact about the passage. Choice D is incorrect because that is just one single fact about the passage. Again, choice B is correct because it encompasses ALL the facts in the passage, not just one single fact.

2. B
Look at the dates in the passage. The shots were fired on April 12 and Congress declared war on April 14.

Choice C is incorrect because the passage states that Lincoln was against slavery. Choice D is incorrect because it never mentions who was or was not at Fort Sumter.

3. B
Choice B matches the rest of the paragraph: a poor family with two children.

Choice A is incorrect because the family is clearly not rich; they are starving.

Choice C is incorrect because, although the family and children are right, the parents are neither happy nor loving.

Choice D is incorrect because the rest of the paragraph shows that they are not royalty. This choice is plausible because of the flow of "a boy and a girl" into the next sentence, but incorrect.

4. C
This flows into the paragraph.

Choice A does not flow into the rest of the paragraph, but is plausible because it mentions the same food. Choice B is incorrect because the rest of the paragraph takes place on an uninhabited island, not in town. Choice D is incorrect because it jumps from talking about their mind-set on the river right into cooking food on the island.

CORRECTION SENTENCES

5. C
Sentence 6 is a fragment. "At least, according to Zach Manchester, the inventor of the nano-satellite KickSat."

This sentence fails to complete the thought, even though it is somewhat consistent with the previous sentence. Sentence 6 does not have a subject and thus does not form any main clause which is essential for constructing a complete thought. This fragment can be revised as "At least, <u>this is</u> according to Zach Manchester, the inventor of the nano-satellite KickSat."

6. B
Suggested changes to Sentence 4 to reduce redundancy, "However, the days when each of us will have our own personal spacecraft are truly not far away!"

The adjectives "own" and "personal" are used simultaneously. Either of them can be used, and the other must be eliminated. The correct form will be either one of the following:

- However, the days when each of us will have our own spacecraft are truly not far away!
- However, the days when each of us will have our personal spacecraft are truly not far away!

7. C
The revised version of sentence 2 is, "In fact, at this point, it seems impossible to think about personal satellites now - just as we once thought about smart phones."

This choice uses the correct punctuation; two commas, one before and one after the subordinate conjunction "at this point" which bridges the adverbial clause after it with the adjective at the start of the sentence. Also the use of a hyphen to express extended thought is correct in choice C.

8. D

The only choice with correct grammar is choice D. It replaces "more tiny" with "tiny" as well as "cubic shaped" with "cube-shaped." Tinier is the correct comparative form of "tiny" and "cubic" is the adjective that must describe the singular noun "shape," not "shapes" or any of its verbal forms. Two word adjectives, such as "a 3-mile race" are hyphenated.

"Under its compact design" is incorrect. Replace with, "with its compact design ... "

9. A

Sentence 4 is least relevant, "Alvin Lee began playing guitar at an early age, and was influenced by his parents' passion for music and inspired by the likes of Chuck Berry and Scotty Moore."

This sentence talks about Lee's source of motivation rather than his achievements, which is actually the main topic of the paragraph. Other sentences are related to a significant extent, but this sentence deviates from the main idea the most.

10. D

The following sentence, if inserted after sentence 11, "With the songs he composed, he established himself as an exemplary figure among fellow guitarists and the immediate generation that followed" best illustrates the main idea of the passage.
This sentence best complements the other sentences and the main idea of the passage which concentrates on the impact Alvin Lee has made on his admirers and contemporaries with his skills and creations. The emphasis of the passage is on how he influenced them with his guitar work and that is complemented best if the sentence by choice D before sentence 11.

Vocabulary

	A	B	C	D	E		A	B	C	D	E
1	○	○	○	○	○	21	○	○	○	○	○
2	○	○	○	○	○	22	○	○	○	○	○
3	○	○	○	○	○	23	○	○	○	○	○
4	○	○	○	○	○	24	○	○	○	○	○
5	○	○	○	○	○	25	○	○	○	○	○
6	○	○	○	○	○						
7	○	○	○	○	○						
8	○	○	○	○	○						
9	○	○	○	○	○						
10	○	○	○	○	○						
11	○	○	○	○	○						
12	○	○	○	○	○						
13	○	○	○	○	○						
14	○	○	○	○	○						
15	○	○	○	○	○						
16	○	○	○	○	○						
17	○	○	○	○	○						
18	○	○	○	○	○						
19	○	○	○	○	○						
20	○	○	○	○	○						

1. Choose the noun that means, self evident or clear obvious truth.

    a. Truism

    b. Catharsis

    c. Libertine

    d. Tractable

2. Choose the best definition for: virago

    a. A loud domineering woman

    b. A quiet woman

    c. A load domineering Man

    d. A quiet man

3. When Joe broke his _____ in a skiing accident, his entire leg was in a cast.

    a. Ankle

    b. Humerus

    c. Wrist

    d. Femur

4. Select another word for the underlined word in the sentence below.

At first I thought she was very rude and boorish, but when I talked to her again she was very <u>genteel.</u>

    a. Chivalrous

    b. Hilarious

    c. Civilized

    d. Governance

5. Choose an adjective that means corrupted, impure.

    a. Adulterate

    b. Harbor

    c. Infuriate

    d. Inculcate

6. Select another word for the underlined word in the sentence below.

Her business success showed that she was very <u>shrewd</u>.

    a. Slow

    b. Astute

    c. Ignorant

    d. Heinous

7. Choose an adjective that means, beyond what is obvious or evident.

    a. Ulterior

    b. Sybarite

    c. Torsion

    d. Trenchant

8. Choose a noun that means, homeless child or stray.

    a. Elegy

    b. Waif

    c. Martyr

    d. Palaver

9. **Select another word for the underlined word in the sentence below.**

His inheritance was very large - a <u>princely</u> sum!

    a. Minor
    b. Tolerable
    c. Large
    d. Pittance

10. **What is the best definition of deprecate?**

    a. Approve
    b. Indifference
    c. Disapprove
    d. None of the above

11. **Choose the best definition for succor.**

    a. To suck on
    b. To hate
    c. To like
    d. Give help or assistance

12. **Select the synonym of conspicuous.**

    a. Important
    b. Prominent
    c. Beautiful
    d. Convincing

13. Select the noun that means eagerness and enthusiasm.

    a. Alacrity
    b. Happiness
    c. Donator
    d. Marital

14. After Lisa's aunt had her tenth child, Lisa found that she had more than twenty _____.

    a. Uncles
    b. Friends
    c. Stepsisters
    d. Cousins

15. Select the word that means benevolence.

    a. Happiness
    b. Courage
    c. Kindness
    d. Loyalty

16. Select the verb that means, to make less severe.

    a. Suspense
    b. Alleviate
    c. Ingrate
    d. Action

17. What is the name of one who gives a gift or who gives money to a charity organization?

   a. Captain
   b. Benefactor
   c. Source
   d. Teacher

18. What is another word for subordinate, or person of lesser rank or authority?

   a. Palliate
   b. Plebeian
   c. Underling
   d. Expiate

19. Choose the best definition of specious.

   a. Logical
   b. Illogical
   c. Emotional
   d. 2 species

20. Choose the best definition of proscribe.

   a. Welcome
   b. Write a prescription
   c. Condemn
   d. Give a diagnosis

21. When Craig's dog was struck by a car, he rushed his pet to the _____.

    a. Emergency room

    b. Doctor

    c. Veterinarian

    d. Podiatrist

22. Choose the best definition of the underlined word. She never made a mistake - her performance was always impeccable.

    a. Charming

    b. Flattering

    c. Perfect

    d. Impervious

23. Select the synonym of boisterous.

    a. Loud

    b. Soft

    c. Gentle

    d. Warm

24. Select the adjective that means hidden, secret, disguised.

    a. Accustomed

    b. Covert

    c. Hide

    d. Carriage

25. Select the verb that means straightforward, open and sincere.

    a. Lawful

    b. Candid

    c. True

    d. Lawful

Answer Key

1. A
Truism: n. self-evident or clear, obvious, truth.

2. A
Virago: Given to undue belligerence or ill manner at the slightest provocation; a shrew, a termagant.

3. D
Femur: n. The bone of the thigh or upper hind limb, articulating at the hip and the knee.

4. C
Genteel: Polite and well-mannered. Stylish or elegant. Aristocratic

5. A
Adulterate: v. To render (something) poorer in quality by adding another substance, typically an inferior one.

6. B
Shrewd: showing clever resourcefulness in practical matters, artful, tricky or cunning, astute, streetwise, knowledgeable

7. A
Ulterior: adj. beyond what is obvious or evident.

8. B
Waif: n. homeless child or stray.

9. C
Princely: In the manner of a royal prince's conduct; large or grand.

10. C
Deprecate: v. To belittle or express disapproval of.

11. D
Succor: v. Aid, assistance or relief given to one in distress; ministration.

12. B
Conspicuous: adj. Standing out so as to be clearly visible..

13. A
Alacrity: adj. Eagerness; liveliness; enthusiasm.

14. D
Cousins

15. C
Benevolent: adj. Well meaning and kindly.

16. B
Alleviate: v. To make less severe, as a pain or difficulty.

17. B
Benefactor: n. Somebody who gives one a gift. Usually refers to someone who gives money to a charity or another form of organization.

18. C
Underling: n. subordinate of lesser rank or authority.

19. B
Specious: adj. Seemingly well-reasoned or factual, but actually fallacious or insincere; strongly held but false.

20. C
Proscribe: v. Denounce or condemn.

21. C
Veterinarian: n. A person qualified to treat diseased or injured animals.

22. C
Impeccable: adj. Perfect, without faults, flaws or errors.

23. A
Boisterous: adj. Noisy, energetic, and cheerful; rowdy.

24. B
Covert: adj. Partially hidden, disguised, secret, surreptitious.

25. B
Candid: adj. Straightforward, open and sincere.

Help with Reading Comprehension

At first sight, reading comprehension tests look challenging especially if you are given long essays to answer only two to three questions. While reading, you might notice your attention wandering, or you may feel sleepy. Do not be discouraged because there are various tactics and long-range strategies that make comprehending even long, boring essays easier.

Your friends before your foes. It is always best to start with passages with familiar subjects rather than those with unfamiliar ones. This approach applies the same logic as tackling easy questions before hard ones. Skip passages that do not interest you and leave them for later.

Don't use 'special' reading techniques. This is not the time for speed-reading or anything like that – just plain ordinary reading – not too slow and not too fast.

Read through the entire passage and the questions before you do anything. Many students try reading the questions first and then looking for answers in the passage thinking this approach is more efficient. What these students do not realize is that it is often hard to navigate in unfamiliar roads. If you do not familiarize yourself with the passage first, looking for answers become not only time-consuming but also dangerous because you might miss the context of the answer you are looking for. If you read the questions first you will only confuse yourself and lose valuable time.

Familiarize yourself with reading comprehension questions. If you are familiar with the common types of reading questions, you are able to take note of important parts of the passage, saving time. There are six major kinds of reading questions.

- **Main Idea**- Questions that ask for the central thought or significance of the passage.

- **Specific Details** - Questions that asks for explicitly stated ideas.

- **Drawing Inferences** - Questions that ask for a logical extension of statements.

- **Tone or Attitude** - Questions that test your ability to sense the emotional state of the author.

- **Context Meaning** – Questions that ask for the meaning of a word depending on the context.

- **Technique** – Questions that ask for the method of organization or the writing style of the author.

Read. Read. Read. The best preparation for reading comprehension tests is always to read, read and read. If you are not used to reading lengthy passages, you will probably lose concentration. Increase your attention span by making a habit out of reading. Read everyday and increase the time slowly each day.

Reading Comprehension tests become less daunting when you have trained yourself to read and understand fast. Always remember that it is easier to understand passages you are interested in. Do not read through passages hastily. Make mental notes of ideas you may be asked.

Reading Strategy

When facing the reading comprehension section of a standardized test, you need a strategy to be successful. You want to keep several steps in mind:

- **First, make a note of the time and the number of sections.** Time your work accordingly. Typically, four to five minutes per section is sufficient. Second, read the directions for each selection thoroughly before beginning (and listen carefully to any additional verbal instructions, as they will often clarify obscure or confusing written guidelines). You must know exactly how to do what you're about to do!

- **Now you're ready to begin reading the selection.** Read the passage carefully, noting significant characters or events on scrap paper or underlining on the test sheet. Many students find making a basic list in the margins helpful. Quickly jot down or underline one-word summaries of characters, notable happenings, numbers, or key ideas. This will help retain information and focus wandering thoughts. Remember, however, that your goal is to find the information that answers the questions. Even if you find the passage interesting, stay on track.

- **Now read the question and all the choices.** Now you have read the passage, have a general idea of the main ideas, and have marked the important points. Read the question and all the choices. Never choose an answer without reading them all! Questions are often designed to confuse – stay focussed and clear. Usually the answer choices will focus on one or two facts or inferences from the passage. Keep these clear in your mind.

- **Search for the answer.** With a very general idea of what the different choices are, go back to the passage and scan for the relevant information. Watch for big words, unusual or unique words. These make your job easier as you can scan the text for the particular word.

- **Mark the Answer.** Now you have the key information the question is looking for. Go back to the question, quickly scan the choices and mark the correct one.

Typically, there will be several questions dealing with facts from the selection, a couple more inference questions dealing with logical consequences of those facts, and periodically an application-oriented question surfaces to force you to make connections with what you already know. Some students prefer to answer the questions as listed, and feel classifying the question and then ordering is wasting precious time. Other students prefer to answer the different types of questions in order of how easy or difficult they are. The choice is yours and do whatever works for you. If you want to try answering in order of difficulty, here is a recommended order, answer fact questions first; they're easily found within the passage. Tackle inference problems next, after re-reading the question(s) as many times as you need to. Application or 'best guess' questions usually take the longest, so, save them for last.

Use the practice tests to try out both ways of answering and see what works for you.

For more help with reading comprehension, see Multiple Choice Secrets at www.multiple-choice.ca

Main Idea and Supporting Details

Identifying the main idea, topic and supporting details in a passage can feel like an overwhelming task. The passages used for standardized tests can be boring and seem difficult - Test writers don't use interesting passages or ones that talk about things most people are familiar with. Despite these obstacles, all passages and paragraphs will have the information you need to answer the questions.

The topic of a passage or paragraph is its subject. It's the general idea and can be summed up in a word or short phrase. Sometimes, there is a short description of the passage if it's taken from a longer work. Make sure you read the description as it might state the topic of the passage. If not, read the passage and ask yourself, "Who, or what is this about?" For example:

> Over the years, school uniforms have been hotly debated. Arguments are made that students have the right to show individuality and express themselves by choosing their own clothes. However, this brings up social and academic issues. Some kids cannot afford to wear the clothes they like and might be bullied by the "better dressed" students. With attention drawn to clothes and the individual, students will lose focus on class work and the reason they are in school. School uniforms should be mandatory.

Ask: What is this paragraph about?

Topic: school uniforms

Once you have the topic, it's easier to find the main idea. The main idea is a specific statement telling what the writer wants you to know. Writers usually state the main idea as a thesis statement. If you're looking for the main idea of a single paragraph, the main idea is called the topic sentence and will probably be the first or last sentence. If you're looking for the main idea of an entire passage, look for the thesis statement in either the first or last paragraph. The main idea is usually restated in the conclusion. To find the main idea of a passage or paragraph, follow these steps:

> 1. Find the topic.
>
> 2. Ask yourself, "What point is the author trying to make about the topic?"
>
> 3. Create your own sentence summarizing the author's point.
>
> 4. Look in the text for the sentence closest in meaning to yours.

Look at the example paragraph again. It's already established that the topic of the paragraph is school uniforms. What is the main idea/topic sentence?

Ask: "What point is the author trying to make about school uniforms?"

Summary: Students should wear school uniforms.

Topic sentence: School uniforms should be mandatory.

Main Idea: School uniforms should be mandatory.

Each paragraph offers supporting details to explain the main idea. The details could be facts or reasons, but they will always answer a question about the main idea. What? Where? Why? When? How? How much/many? Look at the example paragraph again. You'll notice that more than one sentence answers a question about the main idea. These are the supporting details.

Main Idea: School uniforms should be mandatory.

Ask: Why? Some kids cannot afford to wear clothes they like and could be bullied by the "better dressed" kids. Supporting Detail

With attention drawn to clothes and the individual, Students will lose focus on class work and the reason they are in school. Supporting Detail

What if the author doesn't state the main idea in a topic sentence? The passage will have an implied main idea. It's not as difficult to find as it might seem. Paragraphs are always organized around ideas. To find an implied main idea, you need to know the topic and then find the relationship between the supporting details. Ask yourself, "What is the point the author is making about the relationship between the details?"

> Cocoa is what makes chocolate good for you. Chocolate comes in many varieties. These delectable flavors include milk chocolate, dark chocolate, semi-sweet, and white chocolate.

Ask: What is this paragraph about?

Topic: Chocolate

Ask: What? Where? Why? When? How? How much/many?

Supporting details: Chocolate is good for you because it is made of cocoa, Chocolate is delicious, Chocolate comes in different delicious flavors

Ask: What is the relationship between the details and what is the author's point?

Main Idea: Chocolate is good because it is healthy and it tastes good.

Testing Tips for Main Idea Questions

1. Skim the questions – not the answer choices - before reading the passage.

2. Questions about main idea might use the words "theme," "generalization," or "purpose."

3. Save questions about the main idea for last. Questions can often be found in order in the passage.

3. Underline topic sentences in the passage. Most tests allow you to write in your test booklet.

4. Answer the question in your own words before looking at the answer choices. Then match your answer with an answer choice.

5. Cross out incorrect answer choices immediately to prevent confusion.

6. If two of the answer choices mean the same thing but use different words, they are BOTH incorrect.

7. If a question asks about the whole passage, cross out the answer choices that apply to only part of it.

8. If only part of the information is correct, that answer choice is incorrect.

9. An answer choice that is too broad is incorrect. All information needs to be backed up by the passage.

10. Answer choices with extreme wording are usually incorrect. What is most likely Shelly's job?

 a. Musician
 b. Lawyer
 c. Doctor
 d. Teacher

HELP WITH BUILDING YOUR VOCABULARY

Vocabulary tests can be daunting when you think of the enormous number of words that might come up in the exam. As the exam date draws near, your anxiety will grow because you know that no matter how many words you memorize, chances are, you will still remember so few. Here are some tips which you can use to hurdle the big words that may come up in your exam without having to open the dictionary and memorize all the words known to humankind.

Build up and tear apart the big words. Big words, like many other things, are composed of small parts. Some words are made up of many other words. A man who lifts weights for example, is a weight lifter. Words are also made up of word parts called prefixes, suffixes and roots. Often times, we can see the relationship of different words through these parts. A person who is skilled with both hands is ambidextrous. A word with double meaning is ambiguous. A person with two conflicting emotions is ambivalent. Two words with synonymous meanings often have the same root. Bio, a root word derived from Latin is used in words like biography meaning to write about a person's life, and biology meaning the study of living organisms.

- **Words with double meanings.** Did you know that the word husband not only means a man married to a woman, but also thrift or frugality? Sometimes, words have double meanings. The dictionary meaning, or the denotation of a word is sometimes different from the way we use it or its connotation.

- **Read widely, read deeply and read daily.** The best way to expand your vocabulary is to familiarize yourself with as many words as possible through reading. By reading, you are able to remember words in a proper context and thus, remember its meaning or at the very least, its use. Reading widely would help you get acquainted with words you may never use every day. This is the best strategy without doubt. However, if you are studying for an exam next week, or even tomorrow, it isn't much help! Below you will find a range of different ways to learn new words quickly and efficiently.

- **Remember.** Always remember that big words are easy to understand when divided into smaller parts, and the smaller words will often have several other meanings aside from the one you already know. Below is an extensive list of root or stem words, followed by one hundred questions to help you learn word stems.

Here are suggested effective ways to help you improve your vocabulary.

Be Committed To Learning New Words. To improve your vocabulary you need to make a commitment to learn new words. Commit to learning at least a word or two a day. You can also get new words by reading books, poems, stories, plays and magazines. Expose yourself to more language to increase the number of new words that you learn.

- **Learn Practical Vocabulary**. As much as possible, learn vocabulary that is associated with what you do and that you can use regularly. For example learn words related to your profession or hobby. Learn as much vocabulary as you can in your favorite subjects.

- **Use New Words Frequently**. When you learn a new word start using it and do so frequently. Repeat it when you are alone and try to use the word as often as you can with people you talk to. You can also use flashcards to practice new words that you learn.

- **Learn the Proper Usage.** If you do not understand the proper usage, look it up and make sure you have it right.

- **Use a Dictionary.** When reading textbooks, novels or assigned readings, keep the dictionary nearby. Also learn how to use online dictionaries and WORD dictionary. When you come across a new word, check for its meaning. If you cannot do so immediately, then you should write it down and check it when possible. This will help you understand what the word means and exactly how best to use it.

- **Learn Word Roots, Prefixes and Suffixes.** English words are usually derived from suffixes, prefixes and roots, which come from Latin, French or Greek. Learning the root or origin of a word helps you easily understand the meaning of the word and other words that are derived from the root. Generally, if you learn the meaning of one root word, you will understand two or three words. See our List of Stem Words below. This is a great two-for-one strategy. Most prefixes, suffixes, roots and stems are used in two, three or more words, so if you know the root, prefix or suffix, you can guess the meaning of many words.

- **Synonyms and Antonyms.** Most words in the English language have two or three (at least) synonyms and antonyms. For example, "big," in the most common usage, has about seventy-five synonyms and an equal number of antonyms. Understanding the relationships between these words and how they all fit together gives your brain a framework, which makes them easier to learn, remember and recall.

- **Use Flash Cards.** Flash cards are one of the best ways to memorize things. They can be used anywhere and anytime, so you can make use of odd free moments waiting for the bus or waiting in line. Make your own or buy commercially prepared flash cards, and keep them with you all the time.

- **Make word lists.** Learning vocabulary, like learning many things, requires repetition. Keep a new words journal in a separate section or separate notebook. Add any words that you look up in the dictionary, as well as from word lists. Review your word lists regularly.

Photocopying or printing off word lists from the Internet or handouts is not the same. Actually writing out the word and a few notes on the definition is an important process for imprinting the word in your brain. Writing out the word and definition in your New Word Journal, forces you to concentrate and focus on the new word. Hitting PRINT or pushing the button on the photocopier does not do the same thing.

Notice the verbs in bold in the examples above. They are encircling the subjects of each sentence rather than following them. This is inverse word order.

English Grammar and Usage

	A	B	C	D	E		A	B	C	D	E
1	○	○	○	○	○	21	○	○	○	○	○
2	○	○	○	○	○	22	○	○	○	○	○
3	○	○	○	○	○	23	○	○	○	○	○
4	○	○	○	○	○	24	○	○	○	○	○
5	○	○	○	○	○	25	○	○	○	○	○
6	○	○	○	○	○						
7	○	○	○	○	○						
8	○	○	○	○	○						
9	○	○	○	○	○						
10	○	○	○	○	○						
11	○	○	○	○	○						
12	○	○	○	○	○						
13	○	○	○	○	○						
14	○	○	○	○	○						
15	○	○	○	○	○						
16	○	○	○	○	○						
17	○	○	○	○	○						
18	○	○	○	○	○						
19	○	○	○	○	○						
20	○	○	○	○	○						

Part 1 - Punctuation

1. Ted and Janice <u>who had been friends for years went on vacation together</u> every summer.

    a. Ted and Janice, who had been friends for years, went on vacation together every summer.

    b. Ted and Janice who had been friends for years, went on vacation together every summer.

    c. Ted, and Janice who had been friends for years, went on vacation together every summer.

    d. None of the choices are correct.

2. None of us want to go to the <u>party not even</u> if there will be live music.

    a. None of us want to go to the party not even, if there will be live music.

    b. None of us want to go to the party, not even if there will be live music.

    c. None of us want to go to the party; not even if there will be live music.

    d. None of the choice are correct.

3. <u>John, Maurice, and Thomas,</u> quit school two months before graduation.

    a. John, Maurice, and Thomas quit school two months before graduation.

    b. John, Maurice and Thomas quit school two months before graduation.

    c. John Maurice and Thomas, quit school two months before graduation.

    d. None of the choice are correct.

4. "My father said that he would be there on Sunday," Lee explained.

a. "My father said that he would be there on Sunday" Lee explained.

b. None of the choices are correct.

c. "My father said that he would be there on Sunday," Lee explained.

d. "My father said that he would be there on Sunday." Lee explained.

5. I own two dogs, a cat, named Jeffrey and Henry, the goldfish.

a. I own two dogs, a cat named Jeffrey, and Henry, the goldfish.

b. I own two dogs a cat, named Jeffrey, and Henry, the goldfish.

c. I own two dogs, a cat named Jeffrey; and Henry, the goldfish.

d. None of the choices are correct.

6. Choose the sentence below with the correct punctuation.

a. Marcus who won the debate tournament, is the best speaker that I know.

b. Marcus, who won the debate tournament, is the best speaker that I know.

c. Marcus who won the debate tournament is the best speaker that I know.

d. Marcus who won the debate tournament is the best speaker, that I know.

Part II - Sentence Structure and Grammar

Combine the sentences below into one sentence with the same meaning.

7. I hate needles. I want to give blood. I can't give blood.

    a. Although I hate needles, I couldn't give blood even if I wanted to.
    b. Because I hate needles, I can't give blood, although I want to give blood.
    c. Whenever I hate needles, I give blood although I can't give blood.
    d. Whenever I can't give blood, I give blood anyway, although I hate needles.

8. The doctor was not looking forward to meeting Mrs. Lucas. The doctor would have to tell Mrs. Lucas that she has cancer. The doctor hates giving bad news to patients.

    a. The doctor hates giving bad news, so he was not looking forward to meeting Mrs. Lucas and telling her she has cancer.
    b. The doctor has cancer and was not looking forward to meeting Mrs. Lucas and telling her the bad news.
    c. Before the doctor met Mrs. Lucas, he had to give his the patients the bad news that Mrs. Lucas has cancer.
    d. The doctor was not looking forward to giving the bad news to his patients that he had to tell Mrs. Lucas that his patients have cancer.

9. Mom hates shopping. We were out of bread, milk and eggs. Mom went to the supermarket.

a. Because we were out of bread, milk and eggs, Mom hated shopping at the supermarket.
b. Although she hates shopping, Mom went to the supermarket since we were out of bread, milk and eggs.
c. Although we were out of bread, milk and eggs, Mom still hated shopping at the supermarket and went there anyway.
d. Because Mom hated shopping at the supermarket, she went to there to buy her bread, milk and eggs.

10. The ceremony had an emotional <u>affect</u> on the groom, but the bride was not <u>affected</u>.

a. The ceremony had an emotional effect on the groom, but the bride was not affected.

b. The ceremony had an emotional affect on the groom, but the bride was not affected.

c. The ceremony had an emotional effect on the groom, but the bride was not effected.

11. Anna was taller <u>than Luis, but then</u> he grew four inches in three months.

a. None of the choices are correct.
b. Anna was taller then Luis, but than he grew four inches in three months.
c. Anna was taller than Luis, but than he grew four inches, in three months.
d. Anna was taller than Luis, but then he grew four inches in three months.

12. There second home is in Boca Raton, but they're not there for most of the year.

   a. Their second home is in Boca Raton, but there not their for most of the year.

   b. They're second home is in Boca Raton, but they're not there for most of the year.

   c. Their second home is in Boca Raton, but they're not there for most of the year.

   d. None of the choices are correct.

13. Their going to graduate in June; after that, their best option will be to go there.

   a. They're going to graduate in June; after that, their best option will be to go there.

   b. There going to graduate in June; after that, their best option will be to go there.

   c. They're going to graduate in June; after that, there best option will be to go their.

   d. None of the choices are correct.

14. Your mistaken; that is not you're book.

   a. You're mistaken; that is not you're book.

   b. Your mistaken; that is not your book.

   c. You're mistaken; that is not your book.

   d. None of the choices are correct.

15. **You're** classes are on the west side of campus, but **you're** living on the east side.

   a. You're classes are on the west side of campus, but you're living on the east side.

   b. Your classes are on the west side of campus, but your living on the east side.

   c. Your classes are on the west side of campus, but you're living on the east side.

   d. None of the choices are correct.

16. **The Chinese lives in one of the world's most populous nations, while a citizen of Bermuda lives in one of the least populous.**

   a. The Chinese live in one of the world's most populous nations, while a citizen of Bermuda lives in one of the least populous.

   b. The Chinese lives in one of the world's most populous nations, while a citizen of Bermuda live in one of the least populous.

   c. The Chinese live in one of the world's most populous nations, while a citizen of Bermuda live in one of the least populous.

   d. None of the choices are correct.

17. **You shouldn't sit in that chair wearing black pants; I sit the white cat there just a moment ago.**

   a. You shouldn't sit in that chair wearing black pants; I set the white cat there just a moment ago.

   b. You shouldn't set in that chair wearing black pants; I sit the white cat there just a moment ago.

   c. You shouldn't set in that chair wearing black pants; I set the white cat there just a moment ago.

   d. None of the choices are correct.

18. We saw the <u>golden gate Bridge in San Francisco.</u>

　　a. Golden Gate Bridge in San Francisco

　　b. golden gate bridge in San Francisco

　　c. Golden gate bridge in San Francisco

　　d. None of the choice are correct.

Part III - Sentence Completion and Correction

19. Collecting stamps, _____ and listening to shortwave radio were Rick's main hobbies.

　　a. building models
　　b. to build models
　　c. having built models
　　d. build models

20. Every morning, _____, and before the sun comes up, my mother makes herself a cup of cocoa.

　　a. after the kids left for school
　　b. after the kids leave for school
　　c. after the kids have left for school
　　d. after the kids will leave for school

21. Elaine promised to bring the camera _____ at the mall yesterday.

　　a. by me
　　b. with me
　　c. at me
　　d. to me

22. Following the tornado, telephone poles _____ all over the street.

   a. laid
   b. lied
   c. were lying
   d. were laying

Part IV - Grammar – Sentence Correction

23. She is the <u>most cleverest</u> girl in the class.

   a. She is the most clever girl in the class.
   b. She is the cleverest girl in the class.
   c. She is the most cleverer girl in the class.
   d. None of the above.

24. He <u>lived</u> in California since 1995.

   a. He had lived in California since 1995.
   b. He has been living in California since 1995.
   c. He has living in California since 1995.
   d. None of the above.

25. Please excuse <u>me being</u> late.

   a. Please excuse me for late.
   b. Please excuse my being late.
   c. Please excuse my being lateness.
   d. None of the above.

Answer Key

1. A
Use a comma to separate phrases.

2. B
Use a comma separates independent clauses. None of us wants to go to the party, not even if there will be live music.

3. B
Don't use a comma before 'and' in a list.

4. C
Commas always go with a quote and the use of said, explained etc.

5. A
This is an example if a comma which appears before 'and,' but is disambiguating. Without the comma, the sentence would be "I own two dogs, a cat named Jeffrey and Henry, the goldfish." This means there is a cat named Jeffrey and Henry, and a goldfish with no name mentioned. The comma appears to show the distinction.

I own two dogs, a cat named Jeffrey, and Henry, the goldfish.

6. B
Comma separate phrases.

7. A
These three sentences can be combined using 'although,' and 'even if.'

8. A
These two sentences can be combined into one sentence with two clauses separated by a comma.

9. B
These three sentences can be combined using 'although,' and 'since.'

English Usage

10. A
Affect vs. Effect - Affect is a verb (action) and effect is a noun (thing).

11. D
Than vs. Then – Than is used for comparison, as in, taller than, and then is used for time, as in, but then...

12. C
There vs. their vs. they're. There indicates existence as in, "there are." Their is to indicate possession, as in, "their book." They're is the contraction form of "they are."

13. A
There vs. their vs. they're. There indicates existence as in, "there are." Their is to indicate possession, as in, "their book." They're is the contraction form of "they are."

14. C
Your vs. you're. Your is the possessive form of you. You're is the contraction form of you are.

15. C
Your vs. you're. Your is the possessive form of you. You're is the contraction form of you are.

16. A
Singular subjects. "The Chinese" is plural, and "a citizen of Bermuda" is singular.

17. A
Sit vs. Set. Set requires an object – something to set down. Sit is something that you do, like sit on the chair.

18. A
Always capitalize proper nouns.

19. A
Present progressive "building models" is correct in this sentence.

20. C
Past Perfect tense describes a completed action in the past, before another action in the past.

21. D
The preposition 'to' in this sentence means give.

22. C
"Lie" means to recline, and does not take an object. 'Lay' means to place and does take an object. Peter lay the books on the table, or the telephone poles were lying on the road.

23. B
Cleverest is the proper form to express 'most clever.'

24. B
Past perfect continuous, has been living, is proper because the time element, since 1995, and he is still living there now.

25. B
The correct form is, "please excuse me for being late," or, "please excuse my being late."

English Grammar and Punctuation Tutorials

Capitalization

Although many of the rules for capitalization are pretty straight forward, there are several tricky points that are important to review.

Starting a Sentence

Everyone knows that you need to capitalize the first letter of the first word in a sentence, but is it really all that easy to figure out where one sentence starts and another stops? Take these three examples:

That was the moment it really sunk in: There would be no hockey this year.

It was April and that could mean only one thing: baseball.

We played for hours before heading home; everyone felt tired and happy.

In the first example, the first letter after the colon is capitalized while in the second example, it is not. That is because everything after the first example's colon is a complete sentence, while example two's colon there is only one word. In example three you have what could be a complete sentence ("everyone felt tired and happy"), but which is not because it follows a semicolon, making it just another clause instead.

Within a sentence you can have an additional complete sentence if the sentence follows a colon. However, if what could be a complete sentence follows a semicolon, it is a clause and does not get capitalized.

Remember that the same rules apply for quotation marks that apply for colons: A complete sentence inside quotation marks is capitalized, but a single word or phrase is not.

Proper Nouns

The first letter of all proper nouns needs to be capitalized. There are many categories of proper noun. The most common proper nouns are the specific names of people (such as Bill), places (such as Germany) or things (such as Honda Civic). However, there are several less obvious categories of words that should be capitalized as proper nouns.

Historical events such as World War II or the California Gold Rush need to be capitalized.

The names of celestial bodies such as Orion's Belt need to be capitalized.

The names of ethnicities such as African-American or Hispanic need to be capitalized.

Relationship words that replace a person's name such as Mom, Doctor and Mister need to be capitalized. However, this only happens when you use the word to replace the person's name. In the sentence, "My mom went to the store," you do not capitalize it, while in the sentence, "Hey Mom, did you get toothpaste at the store?" you do capitalize it.

Geographical locations are capitalized. This can be tricky because capitalized geographical locations and non-capitalized directions are easy to confuse. Saying, "We drove south for hours," is a direction, so the word "south" should not be capitalized. However, when saying, "While in the United States, we drove to the South to look at Civil War battle fields," you do capitalize the word "South." The difference is that in the first sentence "south" is just the direction you drove. In the second sentence "the South" is a specific region of the United States that formed itself into the Confederacy during the US Civil War.

Proper Adjectives

Proper adjectives are the adjective forms of proper nouns. People from Germany are German; people from Canada are Canadian. German and Canadian are proper adjectives because they are forms of proper nouns that are used to describe other nouns.

Titles of Works

Titles of works are generally capitalized following a specific pattern. Capitalize all the important words in a sentence. Do not capitalize unimportant words such as prepositions and articles.

For example: Alien Spaceship Spotted over Many of the World's Capitals

Notice that the prepositions "over" and "of," and the article "the" are the only non-capitalized words in the sentence.

Punctuation - Colons, Semicolons, Hyphens, Dashes, Parentheses and Apostrophes

Within a sentence there are several different types of punctuation marks that can denote a pause. Each of these punctuation marks has different rules when it comes to its structure and usage, so we will look at each one in turn.

Colons

The colon is used primarily to introduce information. It can start lists such as in the sentence, "There were several things Susan had to get at the store: bread, cereal, lettuce and tomatoes." Or a colon points out specific information, such as in the sentence, "It was only then that the group fully realized what had happened: The Martian invasion had begun."

Note that if the information after the colon is a complete sentence, you capitalize and punctuate it exactly like you would a sentence. If, however, it does not constitute a complete sentence, you don't have to capitalize anything. ("Peering out the window Meredith saw them: zombies.")

SEMICOLONS

Semicolons are super commas. They denote a stronger stop than a comma does, but they are still weaker than a period, not capable of ending a sentence. Semicolons are primarily used to separate independent clauses that are not being separated by a coordinating conjunction. ("Chris went to the store; he bought chips and salsa.") Semicolons can only do this, however, when the ideas in each clause are related. For instance, the sentence, "It's raining outside; my sister went to the movies," is not a proper usage of the semicolon since those clauses have nothing to do with each other.

Semicolons can also be used in lists if one or more element in the list is itself made up of a smaller list. If you want to write a list of things you plan to bring to a picnic, and those things only include a Frisbee, a chair and some pasta salad, you would not need to use a semicolon. However, if you also wanted to bring plastic knives, forks and spoons, you would need to write your sentence like this: "For our picnic I am bringing a Frisbee; a chair; plastic knives, forks and spoons; and some pasta salad."

Using semicolons like this preserves the smaller list that you have in your larger list.

HYPHENS

To join words together to show that they are linked you use hyphens. The most common use of hyphens is to link together words to show that they are working together in a sentence. ("The well-known actor was eating at the table behind us.") This shows explicitly that you are using "well-known" as a single concept and not as two descriptive words in a list.

Hyphens can also be used to split a word in half if you run out of space writing on one line of a page. This is often seen in newspapers and magazines when text is justified to both sides of a page or a column. For example:

> The massive earthquake caused surpris-
>
> ingly little damage in the affected areas.

However, you can only use a hyphen in this way if you split the word between syllables. Often students think that they can use hyphens to break up words wherever they want; this is wrong. For the word "surprisingly" you could have a hyphen between "sur" and "prisingly," "surpris" and "ingly, and between "surprising" and "ly," but nowhere else.

Finally, hyphens can be used to add prefixes to words. This happens a lot in news reports with phrases such as "pro-government troops."

Dashes and Parentheses

Both dashes and parentheses are used to set aside information into parenthetical statements; statements that can be treated as an aside. They do not need to be there for the sentence to make sense, but the information they provide is interesting enough that you feel it should be included. Parentheses are considered stronger than dashes are. (Commas can also be used to separate nonessential information from a sentence, but they are considered to be the weakest of the three.)

As the previous sentence shows, parentheses can surround entire sentences, separating them from the paragraph. Dashes, on the other hand, can separate off the last statement in a sentence. ("Calvin came home and greeted his family for the first time in days—everyone smiled.") Obviously, that last sentence could also be written using a semicolon or as two sentences. The difference is in how you want it to sound to the reader. Should these thoughts be treated as two distinct pieces? Or should everyone smiling at Calvin be part of the main sentence, just separated a bit more strongly—with a slightly longer pause—than a comma could manage?

Apostrophes

There are two primary uses of the apostrophe in English: forming contractions and forming possessive nouns.

Contractions are formed by taking two words and combining them together with an apostrophe replacing the missing letters (do not becomes don't), or by shortening an existing word (cannot becomes can't). Apostrophes can also make contractions by attaching verbs to nouns or pronouns. ("He's going to the store.")

When making singular nouns possessive the general rule is that you add an 's to the end of singular nouns. (This is Tim's bagel.) When dealing with plural nouns that do not end with the letter –s (such as children), the rule is that you also add an 's to the end of the word. (It was the children's favorite movie.) And when dealing with plural nouns that end with the letter –s, you simply add an apostrophe. (My sisters' favorite game is tag.)

However, and this is an important "however" given the controversy it can cause, when dealing with singular words that end with the letter –s (such as circus), there are two standards for how to make them possessive—each with its own grammar books to back it up.

One standard says that you still add an 's to the end of the word. (This is the circus's biggest tent.) The other says that, since the word ends with an –s, it can only get an apostrophe. (This is the circus' biggest tent.) Some style books, such as the Chicago Manual of Style will go so far as to say that the former option is correct, but to avoid inflaming people's passions on the subject, using the latter is perfectly acceptable. The best thing to do is to find out which style the teacher or editor you are writing for at any given time prefers and conform to it for that person.

Commas

Commas are probably the most commonly used punctuation mark in English. Commas can break the flow of writing to give it a more natural sounding style, and they are the main punctuation mark used to separate ideas. Commas also separate lists, introductory adverbs, introductory prepositional phrases, dates and addresses.

The most rigid way that commas are used is when separating clauses. There are two primary types of clauses in a sentence, independent and subordinate (sometimes called dependent). Independent clauses are clauses that express a complete thought, such as, "Tim went to the store." Subordinate clauses, on the other hand, only express partial thoughts that expand on an independent clause, such as, "after the game ended," which you can see is clearly not a complete sentence. (You will learn more about clauses in different lessons.)

The rule for commas with clauses is that a comma must separate the clauses when a subordinate clause comes first in a sentence: "After the game ended, Tim went to the store." But there should not be a comma when a subordinate clause follows an independent clause: "Tim went to the store after the game ended." If you leave the comma out of the first example, you have a run-on sentence. If you add one into the second example, you have a comma-splice error. Also, when you have two independent clauses joined with a coordinating conjunction, you need to separate them with a comma. "Tim went to the store, and Beth went home."

There are some artistic exceptions to these rules, such as adding a pause for literary effect, but for the most part, they are set in stone.

Commas are also used to separate items in a list. This area of English is unfortunately less clear than it should be, with two separate rules depending on what standard you are following. To understand the two different rules, let's pretend you are having a party at your house, and you are making a list of refreshments your friends will want. You may decide to serve three things: 1) pizza 2) chips 3) drinks. There are two different rules governing how you should punctuate this. According to many grammar books, you would write this as, "At the store I will buy pizza, chips, and drinks." This variation puts a comma after each item in the list. It is the version that the style books used in most college English and history courses will prefer, so it is probably the one you should follow. However, the Associated Press style guide, which is used in college journalism classes and at newspapers and magazines, says the sentence should be written like this: "At the store I will buy pizza, chips and drinks." Here you only use a comma between the first two words, letting the word "and" act as the separator between the last two.

Another important place to use commas is when you have a modifier that describes an element of a sentence, but that does not directly follow the thing it describes. Look at the sentence: "Tim went over to visit Beth, watching the full moon along the way." In this sentence there is no confusion about who is "watching the full moon"; it is Tim, probably as he walks to Beth's house. If you remove the comma, however, you get this: "Tim went over to visit Beth watching the full moon along the way." Now it sounds as though Beth is watching the full moon, and we are forced to wonder what "way" the moon is traveling along.

Commas are also used when adding introductory prepositional phrases and introductory adverbs to sentences. A comma is always needed following an introductory adverb. ("Quickly, Jody ran to the car.") Commas are even necessary when you have an adverb introducing a clause within a sentence, even if the clause not the first clause of the sentence. ("Amanda wanted to go to the movie; however, she knew her homework was more important.")

With introductory prepositional phrases you only add a comma if the phrase (or if a group of introductory phrases) is five or more words long. Thus, the sentence you just read did not have a comma following its introductory prepositional phrase ("With introductory prepositional phrases") because it was only four words. Compare that to this sentence with a five word introductory phrase: "After the ridiculously long class, the friends needed to relax."

The last main way that commas are used in sentences is

to separate out information that does not need to be there. For instance, "My cousin Hector, who wore a blue hat at the party, thought you were funny." The fact that Hector wore a blue hat is interesting, but it is not vital to the sentence; it could be removed and not changed the sentence's meaning. Therefore it gets commas around it. Along these lines you should remember that any clause introduced by the word that is considered to provide essential information to the sentence and should not get commas around it. Conversely, any clause starting with the word which is considered non-essential and should not get commas around it.

QUOTATION MARKS

Quotation marks are used in English in a variety of different ways. The most common use of quotation marks is to show quotations either as dialogue or when directly quoting a source in an essay or news article. Fortunately, both of these uses follow the same basic rules.

When you have a quote written as the second part of a sentence, you need to put a comma before the quotation marks and a period inside the quotation marks at the end. (Franklin said, "Let's go to the store.") Conversely, when you have quote as the first part of the sentence with information describing it second, a comma replaces the period at the end of the sentence inside the quotes. ("Let's go to the store," Franklin said.)

If the information in a quote is not a complete sentence, you do not need to capitalize it or put commas around it, if it is not dialogue. (No one thought the idea of "going to the store" sounded very fun.)

Note that when the last word in a sentence has both a quotation mark and a period attached to it, the period is always inside the quotes. This is the case when you have a complete sentence inside a quote ("Let's go to the store."), and when the last word in a sentence just happens to have quote marks around it (Kerri said I was "mean.") You also need to do the same thing with commas. (Kerri said I was "mean," and it made me feel bad.) However, other punctuation marks such as colons, semicolons and dashes do not follow this rule and should come outside the quotes. (Kerri said I was "mean"; it made me feel bad.)

When you want to use a quote inside a quote, you use the standard double-quotation marks for the outer quote and single-quotation marks for the inner quote. ("The sign on the door said 'no soliciting,' so we went to the next house.")

Quotation marks are also used around certain types of titles. To figure out which ones, it helps to look at which titles are not put in quotes as well.

Titles have two categories: large works and small works. Large works are things such as newspapers, magazines, CDs, books and television shows. The defining characteristic of a large work is that it is able to hold small works in it. Small works are the articles inside newspapers and magazines, the songs on a CD, the chapters in a book and the episodes of a television show. It is small works that get quotation marks around them. (Large works, meanwhile, are either underlined or italicized.)

Using quotation marks correctly in a title looks something like this: The two-page article entitled "San Francisco Giants Win World Series" appeared in yesterday's New York Times. The article title is in quotes, and the newspaper title is in italics.

SUBJECT VERB AGREEMENT

Verbs in any sentence must agree with the subject of the sentence in person and number. Problems usually occur when the verb doesn't correspond with the right subject or the verb fails to match the noun close to it.

Unfortunately, there is no easy way around these principals - no tricky strategy or easy rule. You just have to memorize them.

Here is a quick review:

The verb to be, present (past)

PERSON	SINGULAR	PLURAL
First	I am (was)	we are (were)
Second	you are (were)	you are (were)
Third	he, she, it is (was)	they are (were)

The verb to have, present (past)

Person	Singular	Plural
First	I have (had)	we have (had)
Second	you have (had)	you have (had)
Third	he, she, it has (had)	they have (had)

Regular verbs, e.g. to walk, present (past)

Person	Singular	Plural
First	I walk (walked)	we walk (walked)
Second	you walk (walked)	you walk (walked)
Third	he, she, it walks (walked)	they work (walked)

1. Every and Each

When nouns are qualified by "every" or "each," they take a singular verb even if they are joined by 'and'

Examples:

Each mother and daughter *was* a given separate test.
Every teacher and student *was* properly welcomed.

2. Plural Nouns

Nouns like measles, tongs, trousers, riches, scissors etc. are all plural.

Examples:

The trousers *are* dirty.
My scissors *have* gone missing.
The tongs *are* on the table.

3. With and As Well

Two subjects linked by "with" or "as well" should have a verb that matches the first subject.

Examples:

The pencil, with the papers and equipment, *is* on the desk.
David as well as Louis is coming.

4. Plural Nouns

The following nouns take a singular verb:

politics, mathematics, innings, news, advice, summons, furniture, information, poetry, machinery, vacation, scenery

Examples:

The machinery *is* difficult to assemble
The furniture *has* been delivered
The scenery *was* beautiful

5. Single Entities

A proper noun in plural form that refers to a single entity requires a singular verb. This is a complicated way of saying; some things appear to be plural, but are really singular, or some nouns refer to a collection of things but the collection is really singular.

Examples:

The United Nations Organization *is* the decision maker in the matter.

Here the "United Nations Organization" is really only one "thing" or noun, but is made up of many "nations."

The book, "The Seven Virgins" *was* not available in the library.

Here there is only one book, although the title of the book is plural.

6. Specific Amounts Are Always Singular

A plural noun that refers to a specific amount or quantity that is considered as a whole (dozen, hundred, score etc.) requires a singular verb.

Examples:

60 minutes *is* quite a long time.
Here "60 minutes" is considered a whole, and therefore one item (singular noun).
The first million is the most difficult.

7. Either, Neither and Each are Always Singular

The verb is always singular when used with: either, each, neither, every one and many.

Examples:

Either of the boys *is* lying.
Each of the employees *has* been well compensated
Many a police officer *has* been found to be courageous
Every one of the teachers *is* responsible

8. Linking with Either, Or, and Neither Match the Second Subject

Two subjects linked by "either," "or," "nor" or "neither" should have a verb that matches the second subject.

Examples:

Neither David nor Paul *will* be coming.
Either Mary or Tina *is* paying.

Note

If one subject linked by "either," "or," "nor" or "neither" is in plural form, then the verb should also be in plural, and the verb should be close to the plural subject.

Examples:

Neither the mother *nor* her kids *have* eaten.
Either Mary *or* her *friends are* paying.

9. Collective Nouns are Plural

Some collective nouns such as poultry, gentry, cattle, vermin etc. are considered plural and require a plural verb.

Examples:

The *poultry are* sick.
The *cattle are* well fed.

Note

Collective nouns involving people can work with both plural and singular verbs.

Examples:

Nigerians are known to be hard working
Europeans live in Africa

10. Nouns that are Singular and Plural

Nouns like deer, sheep, swine, salmon etc. can be singular or plural and require the same verb form.

Examples:

The swine is feeding. (singular)
The swine are feeding. (plural)

The salmon is on the table. (singular)
The salmon are running upstream. (plural)

11. Collective Nouns are Singular

Collective nouns such as Army, Jury, Assembly, Committee, Team etc should carry a singular verb when they subscribe to one idea. If the ideas or views are more than one, then the verb used should be plural.

Examples:

The committee is in agreement in their decision.

The committee were in disagreement in their decision.
The jury has agreed on a verdict.
The jury were unable to agree on a verdict.

12. SUBJECTS LINKS BY "AND" ARE PLURAL.

Two subjects linked by "and" always require a plural verb

Examples:

David and John are students.
Note
If the subjects linked by "and" are used as one phrase, or constitute one idea, then the verb must be singular

The color of his socks and shoe is black.
Here "socks and shoe" are two nouns, however the subject is "color" which is singular.

PRACTICE TEST QUESTIONS SET 1

The questions below are not the same as you will find on the Corrections Officer - that would be too easy! And nobody knows what the questions will be and they change all the time. Below are general questions that cover the same subject areas as the Corrections Officer. So, while the format and exact wording of the questions may differ slightly, and change from year to year, if you can answer the questions below, you will have no problem with the Corrections Officer exam.

For the best results, take these Practice Test Questions as if it were the real exam. Set aside time when you will not be disturbed, and a location that is quiet and free of distractions. Read the instructions carefully, read each question carefully, and answer to the best of your ability.
Use the bubble answer sheets provided.

Do not attempt more than one set of practice test questions in one day. After completing the first practice test, wait two or three days before attempting the second set of questions.

PRACTICE TEST QUESTIONS 1

CORRECTIONS SITUATIONAL JUDGEMENT

Access 40 Corrections situational judgement questions in the Canada Corrections format online

https://courses.test-preparation.ca/course/sjt

Use Coupon - Sit-Judgement

Includes over 100 BONUS vocabulary question and How to Take a Test tutorial

Sentence Order

	A	B	C	D
1	○	○	○	○
2	○	○	○	○
3	○	○	○	○
4	○	○	○	○
5	○	○	○	○
6	○	○	○	○
7	○	○	○	○
8	○	○	○	○
9	○	○	○	○
10	○	○	○	○
11	○	○	○	○
12	○	○	○	○
13	○	○	○	○
14	○	○	○	○
15	○	○	○	○
16	○	○	○	○
17	○	○	○	○
18	○	○	○	○
19	○	○	○	○
20	○	○	○	○

Practice Test Questions 1

Vocabulary

	A	B	C	D
1	○	○	○	○
2	○	○	○	○
3	○	○	○	○
4	○	○	○	○
5	○	○	○	○
6	○	○	○	○
7	○	○	○	○
8	○	○	○	○
9	○	○	○	○
10	○	○	○	○
11	○	○	○	○
12	○	○	○	○
13	○	○	○	○
14	○	○	○	○
15	○	○	○	○
16	○	○	○	○
17	○	○	○	○
18	○	○	○	○
19	○	○	○	○
20	○	○	○	○

English Grammar

	A B C D E		A B C D E
1	○ ○ ○ ○ ○	21	○ ○ ○ ○ ○
2	○ ○ ○ ○ ○	22	○ ○ ○ ○ ○
3	○ ○ ○ ○ ○	23	○ ○ ○ ○ ○
4	○ ○ ○ ○ ○	24	○ ○ ○ ○ ○
5	○ ○ ○ ○ ○	25	○ ○ ○ ○ ○
6	○ ○ ○ ○ ○	26	○ ○ ○ ○ ○
7	○ ○ ○ ○ ○	27	○ ○ ○ ○ ○
8	○ ○ ○ ○ ○	28	○ ○ ○ ○ ○
9	○ ○ ○ ○ ○	29	○ ○ ○ ○ ○
10	○ ○ ○ ○ ○	30	○ ○ ○ ○ ○
11	○ ○ ○ ○ ○	31	○ ○ ○ ○ ○
12	○ ○ ○ ○ ○	32	○ ○ ○ ○ ○
13	○ ○ ○ ○ ○	33	○ ○ ○ ○ ○
14	○ ○ ○ ○ ○	34	○ ○ ○ ○ ○
15	○ ○ ○ ○ ○	35	○ ○ ○ ○ ○
16	○ ○ ○ ○ ○	36	○ ○ ○ ○ ○
17	○ ○ ○ ○ ○	37	○ ○ ○ ○ ○
18	○ ○ ○ ○ ○	38	○ ○ ○ ○ ○
19	○ ○ ○ ○ ○	39	○ ○ ○ ○ ○
20	○ ○ ○ ○ ○	40	○ ○ ○ ○ ○

Practice Test Questions 1

Sentence Order

Instructions: The first sentence of a paragraph is given below, followed by additional sentences in the paragraph, listed in no particular order. Order the sentences to create the best paragraph. Make sure the paragraph is properly organized and grammatically correct.

1.

A. It could be argued that conscious behaviors - the ones we find easier to recognize and control - represent the real person, and the others are bogus.

B. Nevertheless, those we interact with pick up on and identify our unconscious behavior.

C. These two types of behavior are not necessarily related to each other.

D. Behaviors can be separated into those under our conscious control and those that are not.

    a. DCAB
    b. DACB
    c. DCBA
    d. DABC

2.

A. Due to its nature, the negative stereotypes about race we have inherited from the past are difficult to eradicate completely and reveal themselves in different, more discreet ways.

B. Just like a virus, it adapts to a changing environment.

C. Raising awareness and proper education have certainly decreased racist behaviors.

D. However, racism has been linked to a virus that mutates.

    a. ADBC
    b. CADB
    c. ACDB
    d. CDBA

3.

A. However, modern racists also believe racial equality has been achieved and that we need no further policies to promote equality.

B. The forms of prejudice we live with today have different names, one being Modern Racism.

C. Therefore, modern racism reveals itself at opportune moments, is more oblique than confrontational.

D. Modern racists neither express nor endorse racist views and stereotypes.

    a. BADC
    b. BDAC
    c. DCBA
    d. BDCA

4.

A. Punk is an attitude, an art form, and a music genre, simultaneously accessible and elusive.

B. While punk as a movement formulated in the undercurrents of society, it buoyed to the surface by 1975.

C. It became what it feared, as it laid itself bare and vulnerable to the media and record labels, who would instantly find a way to monetize it.

D. It is something to aspire to while also being the very thing you turn away from in fear that it will be standardized, made mediocre, and destroyed by its self-aggrandizing commercial image.

   a. ACBD
   b. BDAC
   c. BCAD
   d. ADBC

5.

A. This can be the reason that it is currently experiencing a moment of heightened awareness, as it caresses the sensorium and moves toward pleasure, offering calm and refugee from 21st-century storm.

B. That said, the broader sensibility - music of moods, environments, sound as part of the quotidian experience - has its forebears.

C. Ambient is relatively rare in that it's a genre that can be traced back to one artist, and first and foremost, ambient is the creation of Brian Eno.

D. Ambient can also be described as a surprisingly limber, pliable genre, perhaps partly due to its tendency towards self-effacing and anonymous.

   a. ADCB
   b. CBDA
   c. CABD
   d. BADA

6.

A. Rather, historical sources suggest that interest in nature, humanistic learning, and individualism were already present in the late medical period.

B. Renaissance art combined increased awareness of nature, a revival of classical learning, and a more individualistic view of man.

C. However, it became dominant in 15th and 16th-century Italy concurrently with social and economic changes such as the secularization of daily life, the rise of a rational money-credit economy, and significantly increased social mobility.

D. Scholars no longer believe that the Renaissance marked an abrupt break with medieval values, as the French word renaissance suggests, literally 'rebirth.'

    a. BDAC
    b. DBAC
    c. CBAD
    d. DACB

PRACTICE TEST QUESTIONS 1

7.

A. Unlike the previous generation's focus on reason, science, and modern civilization, the Romantics emphasized society's return to nature and living a rustic life.

B. In fact, from a literary standpoint, Romanticism is not related to "romantic" relationships at all.

C. Romanticism in literature refers to much more than hearts and flowers.

D. Instead, literary Romanticism refers to a particular way of viewing nature, literature, society, and individuality.

E. More specifically, they celebrated the uniqueness and impermanence of every human life by living their lives through emotional experiences.

   a. ACDBE
   b. CDBAE
   c. CBDAE
   d. BCDEA

8.

A. Americans also described the negative aspects of the pandemic in greater detail.

B. The researchers have been asking survey questions about Americans' views and reactions to the COVID-19 pandemic over the past year.

C. Nevertheless, for all the difficulties and challenges of the pandemic, most Americans were able to think of at least one silver lining.

D. Across every significant aspect of life mentioned in these responses, a larger share mentioned a negative impact than mentioned an unexpected upside.

    a. DABC
    b. BDCA
    c. BDAC
    d. ADBC

9.

A. More specifically, the pandemic has changed how we work, learn and interact as social distancing guidelines have led to a more virtual existence, both personally and professionally.

B. In less than a year since the virus emerged, it has up-ended day-to-day lives across the globe.

C. To say that the novel coronavirus (COVID-19) pandemic has changed the world would be an understatement.

D. Unsurprisingly, the pandemic has triggered a wave of mental health issues as well.

    a. ACDB
    b. CDAB
    c. BCAD
    d. CBAD

PRACTICE TEST QUESTIONS 1

10.

A. Individuals announce who they are and who they hope to become through appearance style.

B. Fashion became inextricably implicated in constructions and reconstructions of identity.

C. Because the latter are especially susceptible to change, they are prone to fluctuating and fluid ways of understanding oneself in relation to others within the larger context of fashion change.

D. Appearance style is a metaphor for identity that includes physical features as well as clothing and grooming practices.

    a. BDCA
    b. ABDC
    c. BADC
    d. ADVB

11.

A. If you have ever visited a lake, a pond, or even the ocean, then you know about algae.

B. That means they take carbon dioxide out of the atmosphere like plants.

C. Responsible for the green you see on the water, these tiny organisms are not only the foundation of the aquatic food web but also photosynthesize.

D. And we all know how important that is because of global warming.

    a. BDCA
    b. ACBD
    c. CABD
    d. ABAC

12.

A. The choice of what show to watch is unlikely to have life-altering consequences.

B. The way your brain places value on information depends on your personality and preference.

C. If the show got a great review from a critic, that might encourage you to watch it, unless you think that critic has terrible taste in television.

D. However, other decisions can have effects that last the rest of your life.

    a. ACBD
    b. BACD
    c. CBAD
    d. BCAD

13.

A. Risky behavior isn't necessarily bad.

B. Making new friends carries a risk of rejection, but you may actually succeed.

C. Nevertheless, some choices have a risk of more severe consequences, such as experimenting with alcohol, tobacco, or other drugs.

D. Trying out for a team is also risky because you might not get in, but you may still learn a lot from trying.

    a. ADCB
    b. BDAC
    c. ABDC
    d. DBCA

PRACTICE TEST QUESTIONS 1

14.

A. The fact that people are more likely to express their racist views if others support them demonstrates this.

B. You can also use your voice to stand up against it if you feel comfortable.

C. Helping to stop racism is a shared responsibility.

D. To prevent this from happening, it's important always to report online racism when you see it.

    a. DBCA
    b. CADB
    c. ADCB
    d. CDBA

15.

A. Governments and organizations are looking for effective ways to help people escape this kind of poverty.

B. Not having enough money to buy everything we want can be disappointing.

C. Some programs give people cash unconditionally – meaning it is provided with no strings attached.

D. Whereas true poverty is not having enough money for basic human needs like food, clothing, or a place to live.

E. Others give them conditional cash – for example, only if their children attend school.

    a. BDACE
    b. BDAEC
    c. ABCDE
    d. CEDBA

16.

A. You might think that this problem is more prominent in developed countries, where people have higher incomes and consume more energy than they can burn.

B. Obesity has become a big problem worldwide, as it poses many health risks.

C. In fact, developing countries account for 60% of obesity prevalence worldwide.

D. But actually, developing (poorer) countries, where many people suffer from undernutrition, show high rates of obesity as well.

    a. CBAD
    b. ACBD
    c. BADC
    d. BCDA

17.

A. That's why food companies try to sell highly processed foods in developing countries, such as countries in sub-Saharan Africa.

B. These products are very popular among consumers, as they are delicious due to their high content of sugar, fat, and salt and are lower priced.

C. However, this market is saturated in rich countries – the sales can't grow any further.

D. Such popularity makes it a very profitable market.

E. A lot of research shows that one of the main reasons for obesity overall is the consumption of highly processed foods, which provide a lot of energy but few nutrients.

    a. EABDA
    b. EBDCA
    c. BDACE
    d. EDBAD

18.

A. Therefore, you cannot get HIV through sneezes, coughs, talking, or shaking hands.

B. There are a lot of myths about how HIV is transmitted.

C. This can happen through unprotected sex or sharing used needles.

D. HIV spreads when infected blood or body fluids enter the body.

    a. ACDB
    b. DBCA
    c. BCDA
    d. BDCA

19.

A. Antibiotics are miraculous drugs that help us fight off bacterial infections.

B. So, it is essential to study how many antibiotics people consume worldwide.

C. Unnecessary use of antibiotics helps this antibiotic resistance spread faster.

D. However, sometimes bacteria evolve resistance against antibiotic treatment.

    a. ACBD
    b. ADCB
    c. ABCD
    d. CADB

20.

A. T cells are an important part of the immune system.

B. They recognize different infections and protect us from them.

C. Our immune system fights off lots of infections that could harm us.

D. Nevertheless, the numbers of these cells in our body stay the same even when we are old.

E. Our body makes lots of T cells when we are young but slows down production after puberty.

    a. EDCAB
    b. AEDBC
    c. CAEDC
    d. CABED

Practice Test Questions 1

Directions: The following questions are based on several reading passages. A series of questions follow each passage. Read each passage carefully, and then answer the questions based on it. You may reread the passage as often as you wish. When you have finished answering the questions based on one passage, go right onto the next passage. Choose the best answer based on the information given and implied.

Reading

Questions 1 refers to the following passage.

The Life of Helen Keller

Many people have heard of Helen Keller. She is famous because she was unable to see or hear, but learned to speak and read and went onto attend college and earn a degree. Her life is a very interesting story, one that she developed into an autobiography, which was then adapted into both a stage play and a movie. How did Helen Keller overcome her disabilities to become a famous woman? Read on to find out. Helen Keller was not born blind and deaf. When she was a small baby, she had a very high fever for several days. As a result of her sudden illness, baby Helen lost her eyesight and her hearing. Because she was so young when she went deaf and blind, Helen Keller never had any recollection of being able to see or hear. Since she could not hear, she could not learn to talk. Since she could not see, it was difficult for her to move around. For the first six years of her life, her world was very still and dark.

Imagine what Helen's childhood was like. She could not hear her mother's voice. She could not see the beauty of her parent's farm. She could not recognize who was giving her a hug, or a bath or even where her bedroom was each night. Worse, she could not communicate with her parents in any way. She could not express her feelings or tell them the things she wanted. It must have been a very sad childhood.

When Helen was six years old, her parents hired her a teacher named Anne Sullivan. Anne was a young woman who was almost blind. However, she could hear and she could read Braille, so she was a perfect teacher for young Helen. At first, Anne had a very hard time teaching Helen anything. She described her first impression of Helen as a "wild thing, not a child." Helen did not like Anne at first either. She bit and hit Anne when Anne tried to teach her. However, the two of them eventually came to have a great deal of love and respect.

Anne taught Helen to hear by putting her hands on people's throats. She could feel the sounds people made. In time, Helen learned to feel what people said. Next, Anne taught Helen to read Braille, which is a way that books are written for the blind. Finally, Anne taught Helen to talk. Although Helen did learn to talk, it was hard for anyone but Anne to understand her.

As Helen grew older, she amazed more and more people with her story. She went to college and wrote books about her life. She gave talks to the public, with Anne at her side, translating her words. Today, both Anne Sullivan and Helen Keller are famous women who are respected for their lives' work.

1. Helen Keller learned to speak but Anne translated her words when she spoke in public. The reason Helen needed a translator was because

     a. Helen spoke another language.

     b. Helen's words were hard for people to understand.

     c. Helen spoke very quietly.

     d. Helen did not speak but only used sign language.

Practice Test Questions 1

Questions 2 refers to the following passage.

Ways Characters Communicate in Theatre

Playwrights give their characters voices in a way that gives depth and added meaning to what happens on stage during their play. There are different types of speech in scripts that allow characters to talk with themselves, with other characters, and even with the audience.

It is very unique to theatre that characters may talk "to themselves." When characters do this, the speech they give is called a soliloquy. Soliloquies are usually poetic, introspective, moving, and can tell audience members about the feelings, motivations, or suspicions of an individual character without that character having to reveal them to other characters on stage. "To be or not to be" is a famous soliloquy given by Hamlet as he considers difficult but important themes, such as life and death.

The most common type of communication in plays is when one character is speaking to another or a group of other characters. This is generally called dialogue, but can also be called monologue if one character speaks without being interrupted for a long time. It is not necessarily the most important type of communication, but it is the most common because the plot of the play cannot really progress without it.

Lastly, and most unique to theatre (although it has been used somewhat in film) is when a character speaks directly to the audience. This is called an aside, and scripts usually specifically direct actors to do this. Asides are usually comical, an inside joke between the character and the audience, and very short. The actor will usually face the audience when delivering them, even if it's for a moment, so the audience can recognize this move as an aside.

All three of these types of communication are important to the art of theatre, and have been perfected by famous playwrights like Shakespeare. Understanding these types of communication can help an audience member grasp what is artful about the script and action of a play.

2. According to the passage, characters in plays communicate to

    a. move the plot forward

    b. show the private thoughts and feelings of one character

    c. make the audience laugh

    d. add beauty and artistry to the play

Questions 3 - 6 refer to the following passage.

When a Poet Longs to Mourn, He Writes an Elegy

Poems are an expressive, especially emotional, form of writing. They have been present in literature virtually from the time civilizations invented the written word. Poets often portrayed as moody, secluded, and even troubled, but this is because poets are introspective and feel deeply about the current events and cultural norms they are surrounded with. Poets often produce the most telling literature, giving insight into the society and mind-set they come from. This can be done in many forms.

The oldest types of poems often include many stanzas, may or may not rhyme, and are more about telling a story than experimenting with language or words. The most common types of ancient poetry are epics, which are usually extremely long stories that follow a hero through his journey, or ellegies, which are often solemn in tone and used to mourn or lament something or someone. The Mesopotamians are often said to have invented the written word, and their literature is among the oldest in the world, including the epic poem titled "Epic of Gilgamesh." Similar in style and length to "Gilgamesh" is "Beowulf," an ellegy written in Old English and set in Scandinavia. These poems are often used by professors as the earliest examples of literature.

Practice Test Questions 1

The importance of poetry was revived in the Renaissance. At this time, Europeans discovered the style and beauty of ancient Greek arts, and poetry was among those. Shakespeare is the most well-known poet of the time, and he used poetry not only to write poems but also to write plays for the theatre. The most popular forms of poetry during the Renaissance included villanelles, (a nineteen-line poetic form) sonnets, as well as the epic. Poets during this time focused on style and form, and developed very specific rules and outlines for how an exceptional poem should be written.

As often happens in the arts, modern poets have rejected the constricting rules of Renaissance poets, and free form poems are much more popular. Some modern poems would read just like stories if they weren't arranged into lines and stanzas. It is difficult to tell which poems and poets will be the most important, because works of art often become more famous in hindsight, after the poet has died and society can look at itself without being in the moment. Modern poetry continues to develop, and will no doubt continue to change as values, thought, and writing continue to change.

Poems can be among the most enlightening and uplifting texts for a person to read if they are looking to connect with the past, connect with other people, or try to gain an understanding of what is happening in their time.

3. In summary, the author has written this passage

    a. as a foreword that will introduce a poem in a book or magazine

    b. because she loves poetry and wants more people to like it

    c. to give a brief history of poems

    d. to convince students to write poems

4. The author organizes the paragraphs mainly by

   a. moving chronologically, explaining which types of poetry were common in that time

   b. talking about new types of poems each paragraph and explaining them a little

   c. focusing on one poet or group of people and the poems they wrote

   d. explaining older types of poetry so she can talk about modern poetry

5. The author's claim that poetry has been around "virtually from the time civilizations invented the written word" is supported by the detail that

   a. Beowulf is written in Old English, which is not really in use any longer

   b. epic poems told stories about heroes

   c. the Renaissance poets tried to copy Greek poets

   d. the Mesopotamians are credited with both inventing the word and writing "Epic of Gilgamesh"

6. According to the passage, the word that the word "telling" means

   a. speaking

   b. significant

   c. soothing

   d. wordy

CORRECTING SENTENCES

Questions 7 - 10 refer to the following passage

Mankind's thirst for knowledge about ourselves and the universe has always been insatiable, making curiosity a driving force for human advances through history. [1] Not only that, human curiosity and creativity have created countless works

Practice Test Questions 1

of fiction that speculate about future discoveries. [2]

Our neighboring planet Mars, for example, has long led scientists and writers to generate stories about living on the Red Planet. [3] Serious endeavors in science and technology are motivated by our never-ending questions. [4] So far, NASA has carried out several exploratory missions to Mars and the rover robot Curiosity is the latest and most sophisticated. [5]

Curiosity was launched in late November 2011 from Cape Canaveral Air Force Station in Florida. [6] It successfully landed on Mars on August 6, 2012 searching for evidence of life. [7] The car sized robot, weighing about a ton, is equipped with all the technical capacities to carry out its mission to explore our neighbor for biological, geological and geochemical traces of life. [8] It will also test the Martian soil and surface to collect data about its planetary evolution and surface radiation. [9]

Curiosity has been engineered with cutting-edge technologies worth over 2.5 billion US dollars. [10] The most incredible component of the rover is the on-board science lab. [11] Apart from that, it consists of a communications system that allows transmission of commands to the rover from the control centre at NASA, enabling direct control of the robot's activities on the surface of the Red Planet. [12] The Curiosity rover has a number of mounted cameras which assists navigation, as well as capturing images from the Martian surface and transmitting them back to Earth. [13]

7. How would you re-write sentence 1?

   a. No changes

   b. Mankind's thirst for knowledge has always been insatiable, making curiosity a driving factor for human advances through history.

   c. Mankind's thirst for knowledge is insatiable, making curiosity a driving factor for human advances through history.

   d. Humankind's thirst for knowledge is insatiable, making curiosity a driving force in advances throughout history.

8. Which sentence in the third paragraph is least relevant to the main idea of the third paragraph?

    a. 6

    b. 8

    c. 9

    d. 10

9. Which of the following changes would focus attention on the main idea of the last paragraph?

    a. To achieve its goals, Curiosity has been engineered with cutting-edge technologies worth over 2.5 billion US dollars.

    b. Because a lot of funding was available for this project, Curiosity has been engineered with cutting-edge technologies worth over 2.5 billion US dollars.

    c. As there is no guarantee that it will succeed in its mission, Curiosity has been engineered with cutting-edge technologies worth over 2.5 billion US dollars.

    d. NASA's scientific data is so reliable that, being assured of no risk of failure in the mission, Curiosity has been engineered with cutting-edge technologies worth over 2.5 billion US dollars.

10. Which of the following is/are needed in sentence 5?

    a. So far, "NASA" has carried out several exploration missions to Mars and the rover robot Curiosity is the latest and most sophisticated of all.

    b. So far, NASA has carried out several exploratory missions to Mars and the rover robot Curiosity is the latest and most sophisticated of all.

    c. So far, NASA has carried out several exploration missions to Mars and the rover robot -Curiosity- is the latest and most sophisticated of all.

    d. So far, NASA has carried out several exploratory missions to Mars and the rover robot "Curiosity" is the latest and most sophisticated of all.

Green Energy from Olive Oil

Questions 11 - 14 refer to the following passage

The debate over developing sustainable energy sources have been very active in the past two decades. [1] With continued concern over global climate change, environmentalists are urging governments for lowering their dependence on fossil fuels in order for ensuring reduced carbon emission into the atmosphere. [2] Consequently, governments worldwide are turning their attention to the search for non-emissive sources of energy. [3] Renewable substitutes under extensive research are solar power, wind, geothermal energy and harnessing energy from ocean waves. [4]

While the search for environment friendly energy sources is already under way, developing these alternatives at a reasonable cost is a major challenge. [5] No cost-effective replacement for fossil fuels has yet been found. [6] However, recent years have seen remarkable progress in the field of solar energy. [7] Ted Sargent, a Professor at University of Toronto, Canada, has discovered that olive oil has the capacity to capture solar radiation and emit electrons resulting in an electric current. [8] This is a major discovery in the solar power generation industry as it offers a cheap source of harnessing the Sun's energy. [9]

Oleic acid, the main ingredient of olive oil, absorbs infrared radiation is the major component of the Sun's radiation reaching the Earth. [10] The discovery is significant because so far, no attempt has been made to use the abundant infrared radiation we receive throughout the year. [11] Capturing this heat wave radiation, along with the photons that are present in sunlight, increases the efficiency of the solar cells that are already being manufactured commercially. [12] And to make it possible, Professor Sargent has developed a new kind of solar cell called "quantum dots," tiny cells made from gels of tin, bismuth, lead, sulphur and selenium mixed with extra pure olive oil. [13] The resulting ink-like crystal absorbs both photons and infrared radiation and has the capacity to transmit electrons and produce a current. [14]

This new method of capturing the Sun's energy is considered a breakthrough in the solar power industry as it offers cheaper alternatives to the existing use of silicon crystals which are costly to manufacture. [15] And although the invention is yet to prove its efficiency, a lot of funding has already been dedicated to further research. [16]

11. What sentence from the passage is an example of a sentence fragment?

    a. 6
    b. 10
    c. 11
    d. 13

12. Which of the following sentences should be deleted to reduce redundancy?

    a. 5
    b. 6
    c. 9
    d. 15

13. Which of the following changes are needed in sentence 10?

    a. Oleic acid, the main ingredient of olive oil, absorbs infrared radiation is the major component of the Sun's radiation reaching the Earth.

    b. Oleic acid, the main ingredient of olive oil, absorbs infrared radiation, which is the major component of the Sun's radiation reaching the Earth.

    c. Oleic acid, the main ingredient of olive oil absorbs infrared radiation that is the major component of the Sun's radiation reaching the Earth.

    d. Oleic acid, the main ingredient of olive oil, absorbs infrared radiation what is the major component of the Sun's radiation reaching the Earth.

14. Which of the following changes are needed in sentence 2?

a. With continued concern over global climate change, environmentalists are urging governments to lowering their dependence on fossil fuels to ensuring reduced carbon emission into the atmosphere.

b. With continued concern over global climate change, environmentalists are urging governments lower their dependence on fossil fuels in order for ensuring reduced carbon emission into the atmosphere.

c. With continued concern over global climate change, environmentalists are urging governments to lower their dependence on fossil fuels in order for ensuring reduced carbon emission into the atmosphere.

d. With continued concern over global climate change, environmentalists are urging governments to lower their dependence on fossil fuels to ensure reduced carbon emission into the atmosphere.

Hunting Lost Cities from Space

Questions 15 - 18 refer to the following passage

Satellite imaging has become widespread with improvements in telecommunication over the past two decades. [1] Communication satellites in orbit around the Earth have enabled large-scale mapping of the planet's surface which has become freely available thanks to technology giants like Google. [2] Satellite mapping has opened up new possibilities in diverse fields of science and technology. [3]

The key feature of the new tool, according to Professor Sarah Parcak, who discovered many cities, temples and pyramids covered under sands and sediment; is that it offers a wider perspective in size and scale of the location under study. [4] Along with the visual information that the satellite images provide, numerous details about the sites can be obtained from infrared (IR) and gravitational field images. [5] This information, coupled with conventional on-site procedures, are vital for archeology. [6]

IR data collected from satellite imaging provide clues about the activities of humans living in the contemporary times of their civilizations- including their agriculture, vegetation, structures, habitation roads and much more. [7] This type of information is derived from IR imagery which detects IR radiation present in sunlight as it is reflected by the Earth. [8] Different points in a civilization reflect IR radiation in different proportions, revealing the contrast between different areas and provide detailed insight about the causes of these differing heat signatures. [9]

15. Which of the following changes in sentence 6 would focus attention on the main idea of the second paragraph?

    a. These information, along with a supply of some heavy machinery, will help the excavation of every archeological site accomplished within a short period of time.

    b. This information, coupled with conventional on-site procedures, help archaeologists plan their excavation carefully and efficiently.

    c. Such details are valuable records of ancient history and are essential assets of any civilization.

    d. Such details, unfortunately, are available to archeological firms who are willing to invest a lot of money on putting satellites into orbit.

16. Which of the following sentences should be modified to reduce redundancy?

    a. 7
    b. 8
    c. 9
    d. 10

17. Which of the following sentences, if inserted after sentence 3, would best illustrate the main idea of the passage?

   a. The application has inspired archaeologists to use it for searching for the traces of ancient civilizations and other anthropological dynamics.

   b. The new technology will be very useful for excavation of archeological sites.

   c. The application is a breakthrough for archeology and anthropology since it will allows us to zoom into the distant past to look for lost civilizations.

   d. The concept has many positive aspects in the field of archeological science and excavation.

18. Which of the following change(s) is/are needed to sentence 4?

   a. The key feature of the new tool- according to Professor Sarah Parcak, who discovered many cities, temples and pyramids covered under sands and sediment- is that it offers a wider perspective in size and scale of the location under study.

   b. The key feature of the new tool- according to Professor Sarah Parcak- who discovered many cities, temples and pyramids covered under sands and sediment, is that it offers a wider perspective in size and scale of the location under study.

   c. The key feature of the new tool according to Professor Sarah Parcak- who discovered many cities, temples and pyramids covered under sands and sediment- is that it offers a wider perspective in size and scale of the location under study.

   d. The key feature of the new tool, according to Professor Sarah Parcak- who discovered many cities, temples and pyramids covered under sands and sediment is that it offers a wider perspective in size and scale of the location under study.

Malala's Dream

Questions 19 - 20 refer to the following passage

Every child wants to attend school where they can interact, communicate with others and learn the art of life; discover themselves, socialize, have fun and make friends. [1] When they reach adolescence, children start framing their identity by making choices for their future career. [2] It was not so different with Malala Yousafzawi, who was an exemplary student and a responsible daughter since early childhood. [3] She always wanted to be a doctor, and upon entering her secondary school, started to work toward her dream. [4]

However, for girls in such a conservative society, where women's rights have little or no value, achieving such a lofty goal is pretty much impossible, not to mention the many other challenges of living in an unstable country like Pakistan. [5] Add to that an extreme conservative mentality that interferes in anyone's life whose world views do not match theirs. [6]

Malala's dreams were encountered with the obstacles that were also crushing the aspirations of millions of other young girls like her. [7] But unlike others who feared suppression and defamation, Malala stood up for her rights and looked to overcome the challenges facing her. [8] And while doing so, advanced the struggles of all girls like her with similar ambitions. [9] Persuaded by her father, who is a professional educator, she decided to give up her ambition of becoming a doctor and work for the education and establishment of girls in Mingora, a suburban town in Swat District. [10] In doing so, she had to sacrifice her own dreams, believing that at least millions other dreams will be fulfilled at the expense of just one. [1]1

Malala become a professional educator- campaigning for education for girls, side-by-side with her charismatic father who sponsored schools in the district where they live. [12] In the process, she somehow managed to uphold the courage to address the issues facing education for girls and proposed solutions for them. [13] Her sense of leadership soon made her popular among the local girls, and their parents, who supported her in fulfilling the educational rights of girls. [14] At the same time, however, Malala became the target of extremists. [15] She was shot in the head in an assassination attempt while she was returning home from school. [16]

19. Which sentence is not consistent with the author's purpose?

    a. 9
    b. 11
    c. 12
    d. 13

20. Which of the following changes in sentence 10 would focus attention on the main idea of the second paragraph?

    a. Persuaded by her father, who is a professional educator, she sufficed in bearing a mediocre aim of becoming a simple schoolteacher and work for the education and establishment of girls in her locality, Mingora, a suburban town in Swat District.

    b. Instructed by her father, who is a professional educator, she decided to give up her ambition of becoming a doctor and work for the education and establishment of girls in her locality, Mingora, a suburban town in Swat District.

    c. Inspired by her father, who is a professional educator himself, she decided to work for the education and establishment of girls in her locality, Mingora, a suburban town in Swat District.

    d. Contrary to her father, who is a professional educator, she persisted in becoming a doctor and vetoed to leave her father if he turned out to be an obstacle.

VOCABULARY

1. Choose a verb that means fearless or invulnerable to intimidation and fear.

    a. Feeble

    b. Strongest

    c. Dauntless

    d. Super

2. Choose a word that means the same as the underlined word.

I see the differences when they are placed side-by-side and juxtaposed.

    a. Compared

    b. Eliminated

    c. Overturned

    d. Exonerated

3. Choose the meaning of regicide.

    a. v. To endow or furnish with requisite ability, character, knowledge and skill

    b. n. killing of a king

    c. adj. Disposed to seize by violence or by unlawful or greedy methods

    d. v. To refresh after labor

4. Choose the best definition of pernicious.

    a. Deadly

    b. Infectious

    c. Common

    d. Rare

Practice Test Questions 1

5. After she received her influenza vaccination, Nan thought that she was _____ to the common cold.

    a. Immune

    b. Susceptible

    c. Vulnerable

    d. At risk

6. She performed the gymnastics and stretches so well! I have never seen anyone so <u>nimble</u>.

    a. Awkward

    b. Agile

    c. Quick

    d. Taut

7. Are there any more <u>queries</u>? We have already had so many questions today.

    a. Questions

    b. Commands

    c. Obfuscations

    d. Paradoxes

8. Choose a verb that means to remove a leader or high official from position.

    a. Sack

    b. Suspend

    c. Depose

    d. Dropped

9. Choose the best definition of pedestrian.

   a. Rare
   b. Often
   c. Walking or Running
   d. Commonplace

10. Choose the best definition of petulant.

   a. Patient
   b. Childish
   c. Impatient
   d. Mature

11. Paul's rose bushes were being destroyed by Japanese beetles, so he invested in a good _____ .

   a. Fungicide
   b. Fertilizer
   c. Sprinkler
   d. Pesticide

12. Choose the best definition of salient.

   a. v. To make light by fermentation, as dough
   b. adj. Not stringent or energetic
   c. adj. negligible
   d. adj. worthy of note or relevant

13. Choose the best definition of sedentary

   a. n. A morbid condition, due to obstructed excretion of bile or characterized by yellowing of the skin
   b. adj. not moving or sitting at a place
   c. v. To wander from place to place
   d. n. Perplexity

Practice Test Questions 1

14. The last time that the crops failed, the entire nation experienced months of _____.

   a. Famine
   b. Harvest
   c. Plenitude
   d. Disease

15. Choose the best definition of stint.

   a. Thrifty
   b. Annoyed
   c. Dislike
   d. Insult

16. Choose the best definition of precipitate.

   a. To rain
   b. To throw down
   c. To throw up
   d. to snow

17. Choose the verb that means to build up or strengthen in relation to morals or religion.

   a. Sanctify
   b. Amplify
   c. Edify
   d. Wry

18. Choose the noun that means exit or way out.

   a. Door-jamb
   b. Egress
   c. Regress
   d. Furtherance

19. Choose the best definition of the underlined word.

The tide was in this morning but now it is starting to <u>recede</u>.

    a. Go out
    b. Flow
    c. Swell
    d. Come in

20. Choose the word that means private, personal.

    a. Confidential
    b. Hysteric
    c. Simplistic
    d. Promissory

English Grammar, Punctuation, Capitalization and Usage

Directions: Carefully examine the underlined words in the sentences given below. You may see an error in punctuation, grammar, usage or capitalization. Select the correct version of the sentence from the choices given.

1. To make chicken <u>soup; you</u> must first buy a chicken.

    a. To make chicken soup you must first buy a chicken.
    b. To make chicken soup you must first, buy a chicken.
    c. To make chicken soup, you must first buy a chicken.
    d. None of the choices are correct.

Practice Test Questions 1

2. To travel around <u>the globe you have</u> to drive 25,000 miles.

    a. To travel around the globe, you have to drive 25000 miles.

    b. To travel around the globe, you have to drive, 25000 miles.

    c. None of the choices are correct.

    d. To travel around the globe, you have to drive 25,000 miles.

3. The dog loved chasing <u>bones; but never ate them:</u> it was running that he enjoyed.

    a. The dog loved chasing bones, but never ate them; it was running that he enjoyed.

    b. The dog loved chasing bones; but never ate them, it was running that he enjoyed.

    c. The dog loved chasing bones, but never ate them, it was running that he enjoyed.

    d. None of the choices are correct.

4. He had not paid the <u>rent, therefore,</u> the landlord changed the locks.

    a. None of the choices are correct.

    b. He had not paid the rent; therefore, the landlord changed the locks.

    c. He had not paid the rent, therefore; the landlord changed the locks.

    d. He had not paid the rent therefore, the landlord changed the locks.

5. If <u>he would have known</u> about the forecast, <u>he would have postponed</u> the camping trip.

    a. He would have postponed the camping trip, if he would have known about the forecast.

    b. None of the choices are correct.

    c. If he have known about the forecast, he would have postponed the camping trip.

    d. If he had known about the forecast, he would have postponed the camping trip.

6. Although you may not see <u>nobody</u> in the dark, it does not mean that <u>nobody</u> is there.

    a. The sentence is correct.

    b. Although you may not see anyone in the dark, it does not mean that not nobody is there.

    c. Although you may not see anyone in the dark, it does not mean that anyone is there.

    d. Although you may not see nobody in the dark, it does not mean that not nobody is there.

7. He <u>don't</u> have any money to buy clothes and neither <u>does</u> I.

    a. He doesn't have any money to buy clothes and neither do I.

    b. He doesn't have any money to buy clothes and neither does I.

    c. He don't have any money to buy clothes and neither do I.

    d. None of the choices are correct.

Practice Test Questions 1

8. Choose the sentence with the correct grammar.

   a. Because it really don't matter, I don't care if I go there.

   b. Because it really doesn't matter, I doesn't care if I go there.

   c. Because it really doesn't matter, I don't care if I go there.

   d. Because it really don't matter, I don't care if I go there.

9. When we <u>go</u> to the picnic, we will <u>take</u> potato salad and wieners.

   a. None of the choices are correct.

   b. If you come to the picnic, bring potato salad and wieners.

   c. When we go to the picnic, we will bring potato salad and wieners.

   d. If you come to the picnic, take potato salad and wieners.

10. The older children <u>have already eat</u> their dinner, but the baby has <u>not yet ate</u> anything.

   a. The older children have already eat their dinner, but the baby has not yet eaten anything.

   b. The older children have already eaten their dinner, but the baby has not yet ate anything.

   c. The older children have already eaten their dinner, but the baby has not yet eaten anything.

   d. The sentence is correct.

11. Newer cars use <u>less</u> gasoline, and produce <u>less</u> emissions.

a. Newer cars use fewer gasoline, and produce fewer emissions.

b. None of the choices are correct.

c. Newer cars use less gasoline, and produce fewer emissions.

d. Newer cars fewer less gasoline, and produce less emissions.

12. He should have <u>went</u> to the appointment; instead, he <u>gone</u> to the beach.

a. He should have went to the appointment; instead, he went to the beach.

b. He should have gone to the appointment; instead, he went to the beach.

c. None of the choices are correct.

d. He should have gone to the appointment; instead, he gone to the beach.

13. <u>However;</u> I believe that he didn't really try that hard.

a. However, I believe that he didn't really try that hard.

b. However I believe that he didn't really try that hard.

c. None of the choices are correct.

d. However: I believe that he didn't really try that hard.

14. It's important for you to know <u>it's</u> official name; <u>it's</u> called the Confederate Museum.

a. Its important for you to know its official name; its called the Confederate Museum.

b. None of the choices are correct.

c. It's important for you to know its official name; it's called the Confederate Museum.

d. Its important for you to know it's official name; it's called the Confederate Museum.

Practice Test Questions 1

15. Once the chickens had laid their eggs, they laid on their nests to hatch them.

   a. Once the chickens had layed their eggs, they lay on their nests to hatch them.

   b. Once the chickens had lay their eggs, they lay on their nests to hatch them.

   c. Once the chickens had laid their eggs, they lay on their nests to hatch them.

   d. None of the choices are correct.

16. The mother <u>would not of punished</u> her daughter if she <u>could of avoided</u> it.

   a. The mother would not of punished her daughter if she could have avoided it.

   b. The mother would not have punished her daughter if she could of avoided it.

   c. None of the choices are correct.

   d. The mother would not have punished her daughter if she could have avoided it.

17. Even with <u>an</u> speed limit sign clearly posted, <u>a</u> inattentive driver may drive too fast.

   a. Even with an speed limit sign clearly posted, an inattentive driver may drive too fast.

   b. Even with a speed limit sign clearly posted, a inattentive driver may drive too fast.

   c. None of the choices are correct.

   d. Even with a speed limit sign clearly posted, an inattentive driver may drive too fast.

18. Accept for the roses, she did not accept John's frequent gifts.

    a. Except for the roses, she did not accept John's frequent gifts.
    b. Accept for the roses, she did not except John's frequent gifts.
    c. None of the choices are correct.
    d. Except for the roses, she did not except John's frequent gifts.

19. Although he continued to advice me, I no longer took his advise.

    a. Although he continued to advise me, I no longer took his advice.
    b. Although he continued to advice me, I no longer took his advise.
    c. Although he continued to advise me, I no longer took his advise.
    d. None of the choices are correct.

20. To adopt to the climate, we had to adopt a different style of clothing.

    a. To adapt to the climate, we had to adapt a different style of clothing.
    b. To adopt to the climate, we had to adopt a different style of clothing.
    c. To adapt to the climate, we had to adopt a different style of clothing.
    d. None of the choices are correct.

Practice Test Questions 1

21.   When he's <u>between</u> friends, Robert seems confident, but, <u>between</u> you and me, he is really shy.

   a. None of the choices are correct.

   b. When he's among friends, Robert seems confident, but, among you and me, he is really shy.

   c. When he's between friends, Robert seems confident, but, among you and me, he is really shy.

   d. When he's among friends, Robert seems confident, but, between you and me, he is really shy.

22. I will be finished <u>at about</u> ten in the morning, and will be arriving at home <u>at</u> 6:30.

   a. I will be finished at ten in the morning, and will be arriving at home at about 6:30.

   b. None of the choices are correct.

   c. I will be finished at about ten in the morning, and will be arriving at home at about 6:30.

   d. I will be finished at ten in the morning, and will be arriving at home at 6:30.

23. <u>Beside</u> the red curtains and pillows, there was a red rug <u>besides</u> the couch.

   a. Beside the red curtains and pillows, there was a red rug beside the couch.

   b. Besides the red curtains and pillows, there was a red rug beside the couch.

   c. Besides the red curtains and pillows, there was a red rug besides the couch.

   d. None of the choices are correct.

24. Although John <u>may</u> swim very well, the lifeguard <u>may</u> not allow him to swim in the pool.

    a. Although John can swim very well, the lifeguard may not allow him to swim in the pool.

    b. None of the choices are correct.

    c. Although John can swim very well, the lifeguard can not allow him to swim in the pool.

    d. Although John may swim very well, the lifeguard may not allow him to swim in the pool.

25. Her <u>continuous</u> absences caused a <u>continuous</u> disruption at the office.

    a. Her continuous absences caused a continual disruption at the office.

    b. Her continual absences caused a continuous disruption at the office.

    c. Her continual absences caused a continual disruption at the office.

    d. None of the choices are correct.

26. During the famine, the Irish people had to <u>immigrate</u> to other countries; many of them <u>immigrated</u> to the United States.

    a. During the famine, the Irish people had to emigrate to other countries; many of them immigrated to the United States.

    b. None of the choices are correct.

    c. During the famine, the Irish people had to emigrate to other countries; many of them emigrated to the United States.

    d. During the famine, the Irish people had to immigrate to other countries; many of them emigrated to the United States.

Practice Test Questions 1

27. His home was <u>further</u> than we expected; <u>further</u>, the roads were very bad.

    a. His home was farther than we expected; farther, the roads were very bad.

    b. His home was farther than we expected; further, the roads were very bad.

    c. None of the choices are correct.

    d. His home was further than we expected; farther, the roads were very bad.

28. The volunteers brought groceries and toys to the homeless shelter; the latter was given to the staff, while the groceries were given directly to the children.

    a. The volunteers brought groceries and toys to the homeless shelter; the latter were given to the staff, while the former were given directly to the children.

    b. The volunteers brought groceries and toys to the homeless shelter; the former was given to the staff, while the latter was given directly to the children.

    c. The volunteers brought groceries and toys to the homeless shelter; the groceries were given to the staff, while the former was given directly to the children.

    d. None of the choices are correct.

29. You shouldn't <u>sit</u> in that chair wearing black pants; I <u>sit</u> the white cat there just a moment ago.

    a. You shouldn't sit in that chair wearing black pants; I set the white cat there just a moment ago.

    b. You shouldn't set in that chair wearing black pants; I sit the white cat there just a moment ago.

    c. You shouldn't set in that chair wearing black pants; I set the white cat there just a moment ago.

    d. None of the choices are correct.

30. Mars is the god of war.

    a. Mars is the god or war.
    b. Mars is the God of war.
    c. Mars is the God of War.
    d. None of the choices are correct.

31. This is her third term as <u>Mayor of chicago</u>.

    a. This is her third term as mayor of Chicago.
    b. This is her third term as Mayor of Chicago.
    c. This is her third term as mayor of chicago.
    d. None of the above.

32. I was able to speak with Susan Roberts <u>mayor of tampa</u>.

    a. I was able to speak with Susan Roberts, Mayor of Tampa.

    b. I was able to speak with Susan Roberts, mayor of Tampa.

    c. I was able to speak with Susan Roberts, Mayor of tampa.

    d. None of the Above.

33. I think <u>thanksgiving</u> is the best <u>Fall Holiday</u>.

    a. I think thanksgiving is the best fall holiday.

    b. I think Thanksgiving is the best Fall holiday.

    c. I think Thanksgiving is the best fall holiday.

    d. None of the above.

34. I will be skipping The Fall 2013 semester.

    a. I will be skipping the Fall 2013 Semester.

    b. I will be skipping the fall 2013 semester.

    c. I will be skipping the Fall 2013 semester.

    d. None of the above.

35. The man was asked to come with her daughter and his test results.

    a. The man was asked to come with his daughter and her test results.

    b. The man was asked to come with her daughter and her test results.

    c. The man was asked to come with her daughter and our test results.

    d. None of the above.

Answer Key

Sentence Order

1. C
First, decide on the opening sentence and the last sentence. Here, the first sentence is D as it introduces a topic. Then comes C as the word 'these two' progresses the information in D. The topic is further developed in sentence Lastly, B includes a connecting word (nevertheless), which contradicts the previous sentence that although only conscious behavior is considered real, we notice unconscious ones as well.

Tip: Look for the transitions and connecting words as they give you a hint about the order of the sentence—for example, these and nevertheless in this case.

2. D
First, decide on the opening sentence and the last sentence. Here, the first sentence is C as it introduces a topic, and all the other sentences contain either a connecting word or a transition. Then comes D, as it contradicts C that although racist behavior has decreased, there is something that should be considered. Then B as it specifies the information in C. Lastly, the last one is A, which explains what the metaphor of 'mutating virus' stands for.

3. B
First, decide on the opening sentence and the last sentence. Here, the first sentence is B as it introduces a topic - Modern Racism. Then comes D as it provides a piece of further information about the topic, that modern racists don't show any kind of racist behaviors. Then A as it contradicts the information in D that despite the fact that they don't show racist behaviors, they think it's not a current issue of society. Lastly, the last one is C, which is a logical development of the previously stated information that modern racism is not expressed in action and is hidden.

PRACTICE TEST QUESTIONS 1

4. D
First, decide on the opening sentence and the last sentence. Here, the first sentence is A as it introduces a topic - punk, and all the other sentences contain either a connecting word or a transition. Then comes D, as it describes one of the aspects of the term. Sentence C definitely is the progress of sentence B as it explains that as the punk movement buoyed on the surface, it became the very thing it wasn't supposed to evolve to. So in the correct sequence, D will be followed by B, and the last one will be C.

5. B
First, decide on the opening sentence and the last sentence. Here, the first sentence is C as it introduces a topic - Genre of Ambient, and all the other sentences contain either a connecting word or a transition. Then comes B as it contrasts C. Sentence A is the progress of sentence D as it starts with 'this,' which refers to the description provided in D.

6. A
First, decide on the opening sentence and the last sentence. Here, the first sentence is B as it introduces a topic - Renaissance. Sentences D, A, C create a sequence. Sentence A contains the different idea of the common belief provided in D. Then, sentence C contradicts this idea by emphasizing that although humanism and individualism existed before the Renaissance, they became dominant during that period.

7. C
First, find the opening sentence. Here, it's C as it sets the general topic. All the other sentences contain some kind of transition words, and you need to figure out the order. C should be followed by B and D as they develop the idea that Romanticism is not related to 'romantic' (B) and then define it (D). Words "in fact' and 'instead' should help you find the right direction. Sentence E specifies something. The information in E connects Romanticism to emotions which is more logical to be the development of sentence A which contrasts Romanticism to science and reason. Additionally, the pronoun 'they' in sentence E refers to Romantics mentioned earlier.

8. C

First, find the opening sentence, which is B, as all the others contain transition words. Then comes D, as it briefly summarizes the results of the research. A adds a specification of these responses, and lastly, C contrasts these results that some positive changes were mentioned as well.

9. D

The opening sentence will be C as it's the only sentence where Coronavirus (COVID-19) is mentioned, so it introduces the topic. Then the most logical development will be B which states that everyday life was changed for everyone and is specified in sentence D adds one of the important aspects which also was affected by the virus.

10. C

The first sentence should be B as it sets the topic. It is developed in sentence A and the new term of 'appearance style' is introduced. D defines the new term, and then sentence C gives some details of one of its aspects.

11. B

The opening sentence is A as it introduces the algae. Then algae are described in sentence C. 'That means' in sentence B is referring to information in C. Closing sentence is D as it reckons the whole sequence.

12. D

The first sentence should be B as it describes the brain mechanism. It's followed by C, which is an example of the topic in sentence B. A gives value to this example, and then sentence D provides a contrast by stating that the exact mechanism can be very harmful as well.

13. C

The opening sentence should be A, as all the other sentences contain transition words. B and D both are examples of risky behaviors that are not necessarily bad. However, sentence D includes the word 'also,' indicating that it should follow B. Sentence C contradicts this idea by naming some risky behaviors that might have negative consequences.

Practice Test Questions 1

14. B
The opening sentence is C, as all the others contain transitions. The only sentence that can be a logical development of this is D is a response to A as it provides a way to prevent online racism by reporting it. B adds an option that can be done together with reporting.

15. A
The opening sentence is B, as it is the only sentence that doesn't contain transition words. Then comes D as it introduces the contradictory thought of what true poverty is. D is followed by A - 'this kind of poverty' gives a hint for that. Then comes C and E as they describe two methods of how government and organizations help people in poverty.

16. C
The first sentence is B as it introduces the topic - the problem of obesity. The following sentence can only be A, and 'this problem is more prominent' also gives a hint. Following sentences are D, and C. D shows that the reality is different than what one might think, and C specifies that it is contrary to that thought.

17. B
The opening sentence is E as it's the only one not containing the transition word and it introduces the subjects as well. The comes B, which explains why highly processed food is so desirable. The following one is D, 'such popularity' can be a hint for this. Then comes C as it opposites D that this market can't grow further in rich countries and lastly A, which explains why such food is mainly sold in developing countries.

18. D
The opening sentence can be either B or D. However, sentence B is more general and introduces the topic more broadly, whereas D is concentrated on more specified information. A is followed by D, and then C, which gives more details on the topic in D. It also contains the transition word 'this' as a hint. Lastly, A gives the conclusion that HIV is not transmitted through sneezes, coughs, etc.

19. B

The opening sentence is A as it sets the subject. Then comes D, as it shows the other side of bacteria and antibiotics. This is followed by C, which contains a hint word 'this.' The last sentence is B as it gives a conclusion.

20. D

The first sentence is C as it sets the general topic. Then comes A as it narrows down the immune system to just T cells. Then B describes T cells. Following sentences are E and D. 'Nevertheless' in D gives a hint that it contradicts something.

Reading

1. A

The correct answer because that fact is stated directly in the passage. The passage explains that Anne taught Helen to hear by allowing her to feel the vibrations in her throat.

2. D

This question tests the reader's summarization skills. The question is asking very generally about the message of the passage, and the title, "Ways Characters Communicate in Theatre," is one indication of that. The other choices A, B, and C are all directly from the text, and therefore readers may be inclined to select one of them, but are too specific to encapsulate the entirety of the passage and its message.

3. C

This question tests the reader's summarization skills. The use of the word "actually" in describing what kind of people poets are, as well as other moments like this, may lead readers to selecting Choices B or D, but the author is more informing than trying to persuade readers. The author gives no indication that she loves poetry (choice B) or that people, students specifically (D), should write poems. Choice A is incorrect because the style and content of this paragraph do not match those of a foreword; forewords usually focus on the history or ideas of a specific poem to introduce it more fully and help it stand out against other poems. The author here focuses on several poems and gives broad statements. Instead, she tells a kind of story about poems, giving three very broad time periods in which to discuss them, thereby giving a brief history of poetry, as choice C states.

4. A

This question tests the reader's summarization skills. Key words in the topic sentences of each of the paragraphs ("oldest," "Renaissance," "modern") should give the reader an idea that the author is moving chronologically. The opening and closing sentence-paragraphs are broad and talk generally. B seems reasonable, but epic poems are mentioned in two paragraphs, eliminating the idea that only new types of poems are used in each paragraph. Choice C is also easily eliminated because the author clearly mentions several different poets, groups of people, and poems. Choice D also seems reasonable, considering that the author does move from older forms of poetry to newer forms, but use of "so (that)" makes this statement false, for the author gives no indication that she is rushing (the paragraphs are about the same size) or that she prefers modern poetry.

5. D

This question tests the reader's attention to detail. The key word is "invented"--it ties together the Mesopotamians, who invented the written word, and the fact that they, as the inventors, also invented and used poetry. The other selections focus on other details mentioned in the passage, such as that the Renaissance's admiration of the Greeks (choice C) and that Beowulf is in Old English (choice A). Choice B may seem like an attractive answer because it is unlike the others and because the idea of heroes seems rooted in ancient and early civilizations.

6. B

This question tests the reader's vocabulary and contextualization skills. "Telling" is not an unusual word, but it may be used here in a way that is not familiar to readers, as an adjective rather than a verb in gerund form. A may seem like the obvious answer to a reader looking for a verb to match the use they are familiar with. If the reader understands that the word is being used as an adjective and that choice A is a ploy, they may opt to select choice D, "wordy," but it does not make sense in context. Choice C can be easily eliminated, and doesn't have any connection to the paragraph or passage. "Significant" (choice B) makes sense contextually, especially relative to the phrase "give insight" used later in the sentence.

CORRECTING SENTENCES

7. D
Suggested revision of sentence 1, "Humankind's thirst for knowledge is insatiable, making curiosity a driving force for advances throughout history."

Use the gender neutral "humankind. Replace the past perfect "has always been" with the present tense to make a simpler and more direct sentence. "Though history" is incorrect. Use "throughout" when referring to a time period. Replace the preposition "for" with "in."

8. A
Sentence 6 is the least relevant. "Curiosity was launched in late November 2011 from Cape Canaveral Air Force Station in Florida."

The third paragraph talks about the objectives of the rover. All sentences other than sentence 7 mention the objectives. This sentence, however, informs about when the spacecraft was launched.

9. A
Sentence 10 is least relevant to the main idea of the third paragraph. The following changes are suggested, "<u>To achieve its goals</u>, Curiosity has been engineered with cutting-edge technologies worth a budgetary expense exceeding 2.5 billion US dollars."

Clearly, the last paragraph talks about how Curiosity has been engineered to accomplish its objectives. The previous paragraph addressing the objectives of the rover, addition of the phrase "To achieve its goals," in choice A, acts as a transition sentence between the paragraphs.

10. D
The changes needed to sentence 5 are, "So far, NASA has carried out several exploratory missions to Mars and the rover robot "Curiosity" is the latest and most sophisticated of all."

"Curiosity" is the name of a spacecraft that was assigned the particular name because of its association of its mission to satisfy our curiosity about the planet Mars. In this respect, the name bears a special meaning and emphasis, which must be reflected in representing it using the quotation mark.

Use of the adjective "exploratory" to describe the missions is correct.

Choice D offers these changes.

11. C
Sentence 11 is a fragment. "The discovery is significant because so far, no attempt has been made to use the abundant infrared radiation we receive throughout the year."

The fragment contains a subordinate clause derived from the complete thought "The discovery is significant because so far no attempt has been made to make use of the infra-red radiation that we receive in an abundant supply throughout the year." It also contains the subject of the main clause, "The discovery," but does not have any verbal phrase for the main clause. Since the main clause remains incomplete, the thought is expressed in part. Therefore, it is a sentence fragment.

12. C
Sentence 9 can be deleted to reduce redundancy. "This is a major discovery in the solar power generation industry as it offers a cheap source of harnessing the Sun's energy."

Sentence 9 contributes to double redundancy; that is, it repeats two separate ideas. Along with repeating the cost-effective characteristic of the new discovery, it also reiterates the fact that it is a major discovery, both of which are unnecessary. It also interferes in the paragraph transition which can be established between sentence 8 and 10 if it is removed.

13. B
Suggested corrections to sentence 10, "Oleic acid, the main ingredient of olive oil, absorbs infra-red radiation, which is the major component of the Sun's radiation reaching the Earth."
The sentence is missing the subordinate conjunction "which" or "that" necessary to construct the subordinate clause, with a comma before "which." Choices B and C suggest these changes, but since choice C contains a punctuation error,

only B is has the valid answer.

14. D

Suggested changes to sentence 2, "With continued concern over global climate change, environmentalists are urging governments to lower their dependence on fossil fuels to ensure reduced carbon emission into the atmosphere."

This sentence contains inappropriate use of gerunds and infinitives. To-infinitives are preferred when the continuous form of a main verb is used right before or after them. Here,, "urging" should be followed by the to-infinitive of "lower." Further across the sentence, the linking phrase "to," has only one acceptable form; itself. Therefore, the verb which is linked to must contain the infinitive form. The gerund form must be discarded. The only valid choice is D.

15. B

Suggested changes to sentence 6 are, "This information, coupled with conventional on-site procedures, help archaeologists plan their excavation carefully and efficiently."

The second paragraph points out the significance of satellite imaging for archeological studies. The original sentence only makes a general claim. Choice A contradicts excavation principles by adding "along with a supply of heavy machinery" which would destroy the site. Choice B, more appropriately, adds the aspects of archeological excavation that are going to be boosted by the technology. Choices C and D offer very little relevance to satellite imaging and the dimensions of excavation that are going to be affected.

16. C

Sentence 9 can be re-written, "Different points in a civilization reflect IR radiation differently, provide detailed insight about the causes of these differing heat signatures."

This is a shorter and more concise sentence which eliminates some details.

17. A

The following sentence, inserted after sentence 3, would best illustrate the main idea, "The application has inspired archaeologists to use it for searching for the traces of ancient civilizations and other anthropological dynamics."

Choice A points out the significance of the application with some details that are addressed in the subsequent paragraphs. All other choices are either too general or less relevant to the main idea of the passage.

18. A
Suggested changes to sentence 4 are, "The key feature of the new tool- according to Professor Sarah Parcak, who discovered many cities, temples and pyramids covered under sands and sediment- is that it offers a wider perspective in size and scale of the location."

The changes in this sentence are related to punctuation. The original sentence contains a semicolon before a verbal phrase which is not justifiable with its standard use. The sentence can be modified using parenthetic dashes since using parenthetic commas makes the sentence very complicated as the sentence contains several clauses and a list.

19. D
Sentence 13 is not consistent with the author's purpose. "In the process, she somehow managed to uphold the courage to address the issues facing education for girls and proposed solutions for them."

This sentence, ironically contrasts the character of the passage, and in a way belittles Malala's efforts to address the issues facing girls education, particularly with the words "somehow," "managed" and "uphold." This is, to a great extent, inconsistent with the author's appreciation of Malala.

20. C
Suggested changes to sentence 10 to focus attention on the main idea are, "Inspired by her father, who is an professional educator himself, she decided to work for the education and establishment of girls in her locality, Mingora, a suburban town in Swat District."

The second paragraph discusses the challenges facing Malala and young girls like her. It fine-tunes the reason why Malala had to change her ambition even though she is a talented and successful student; showing that she actually did not give up on her ambition, but rather sacrificed it for materializing others'. In this sense, her father was a role model from whom she could receive inspiration only; not persuasion, instruction or contradiction- for making up her mind to be an professional educator like him. Therefore, choices A, B and D are not relevant. Choice C focuses on the main idea.

Vocabulary

1. C
Dauntless: adj. Invulnerable to fear or intimidation.

2. A
Juxtaposed: adj. Placed side-by-side often for comparison or contrast.

3. B
Regicide: v. killing of a king.

4. A
Pernicious: adj. Causing much harm in a subtle way.

5. A
Immune: adj. Resistant to a particular infection or toxin owing to the presence of specific antibodies.

6. B
Nimble: adj. Quick and light in movement or action.

7. A
Queries: n. Questions or inquiries.

8. C
Depose: To remove (a leader) from (high) office, without killing the incumbent.

9. D
Pedestrian: Ordinary, dull; everyday; unexceptional.

10. B
Petulant: adj. Childishly irritable.

11. D
Pesticide: n. A substance used for destroying insects or other organisms harmful to cultivated plants or to animals.

Practice Test Questions 1

12. D
Salient: adj. worthy or note or relevant.

13. B
Sedentary: adj. not moving or sitting in one place.

14. A
Famine: n. extreme scarcity of food.

15. A
Stint: n. To be sparing.

16. A
Precipitate: v. to rain.

17. C
Edify: v. To instruct or improve morally or intellectually.

18. B
Egress: n. An exit or way out.

19. A
Recede: v. To move back, to move away.

20. A
Confidential: adj. kept secret within a certain circle of persons; not intended to be known publicly.

English Language Arts

1. C
Comma separate phrases.

2. D
The comma separates clauses and numbers are separated with a comma. The correct sentence is,
'To travel around the globe, you have to drive 25,000 miles.'

3. A
The dog loved chasing bones, but never ate them; it was running that he enjoyed.

4. B
The semicolon links independent clauses with a conjunction (therefore).

5. D
The third conditional is used for talking about an unreal situation (that did not happen) in the past. For example, "If I had studied harder, [if clause] I would have passed the exam [main clause]. Which is the same as, "I failed the exam, because I didn't study hard enough."

6. C
Double negative sentence. In double negative sentences, one negative is replaced with "any."

7. A
Disagreeing with a negative statement uses "neither." Disagreeing with a negative statement uses "neither." Use "I do" and "He does."

8. C
Doesn't, does not, or does is used with the third person singular--words like he, she, and it. Don't, do not, or do is used for other subjects.

Practice Test Questions 1

9. C
Bring vs. Take. Usage depends on your location. Something coming your way is brought to you. Something going away is taken from you.

10. C
Present perfect. You cannot use the Present Perfect with specific time expressions such as: yesterday, one year ago, last week, when I was a child, at that moment, that day, one day, etc. The Present Perfect is used with unspecific expressions such as: ever, never, once, many times, several times, before, so far, already, yet, etc.

11. C
Fewer vs. Less. 'Fewer' is used with countables and 'less' is used with uncountables.

12. B
Went vs. Gone. Went is the simple past tense. Gone is used in the past perfect.

13. A
When using 'however,' place a comma before and after, except when however begins the sentence.

14. C
Its vs. It's. 'It's' is a contraction for it is or it has. 'Its' is a possessive pronoun meaning, more or less, of it or belonging to it.

15. C
Lay vs. Lie. Lie requires an object and lay does not. Laid is the past tense of lay.

16. D
The third conditional is used for talking about an unreal situation (that did not happen) in the past. For example, "If I had studied harder, [if clause] I would have passed the exam [main clause]. Which is the same as, "I failed the exam, because I didn't study hard enough."

17. D
A vs. An. The article 'a' come before a consonant and 'an' comes before a vowel.

18. A
Accept vs. Except. To accept is to receive or to say yes. Except is a preposition that means excluding.

19. A
Advise vs. Advice. To advise is to give advice. Advice is an opinion that someone offers.

20. C
Adapt vs. Adopt.
Adapt means "to change." Usually we adapt to someone or something. Adopt means "to take as one's own."

21. D
Among vs. Between. 'Among' is for more than 2 items, and 'between' is only for 2 items.

When he's among friends (many or more than 2), Robert seems confident, but, between you and me (two), he is very shy.

22. D
At vs. About. At refers to a specific time and about refers to a more general time. A common usage is 'at about 10,' but it isn't proper grammar.

23. B
Beside vs. Besides. 'Beside' means next to, and 'besides' means in addition to.

24. A
Can vs. May. 'Can' refers to ability and 'may' refers to permission.

Although John can swim (is able to. very well, he may not (permission) be allowed to swim in the pool.

25. B
Continual vs. Continuous. 'Continuous' means a time with no interruption and 'continual' means a time with interruption.

Practice Test Questions 1

Her continual absences (with interruption – not always absent) caused a continuous disruption (the disruption was ongoing without interruption) at the office.

26. A
Emigrate vs. Immigrate. To emigrate means to leave one's country and to immigrate means to come to a country.

27. B
Further vs. Farther. 'Farther' is used for physical distance, and 'further' is used for figurative distance.

28. B
Former vs. Latter. 'Former' refers to the first of two things, 'latter' to the second.

29. A
Sit vs. Set. 'Set' requires an object – something to set down. 'Sit' is something that you do, like sit on the chair.

30. C
The names of God, specific deities, religious figures, and holy books are capitalized.

31. B
Capitalize a title when used with a name or other noun. So, The Mayor of Chicago is capitalized, whereas "he spoke to the mayor" is not.

32. B
Titles preceding names are capitalized, but not titles that follow names.

33. C
Holidays are capitalized, the names of seasons are not.

34. C
The names of seasons are not capitalized because they are generic nouns. If a season is used in a title, such as the "Fall 2012 semester," Fall 2012 is a title and capitalized.

35. A
A Pronoun should conform to its antecedent in gender, number and person.

PRACTICE TEST QUESTIONS SET 2

THE PRACTICE TEST PORTION PRESENTS QUESTIONS THAT ARE REPRESENTATIVE OF THE TYPE OF QUESTION YOU SHOULD EXPECT TO FIND ON THE CORRECTIONS OFFICER EXAM. HOWEVER, THEY ARE NOT INTENDED TO MATCH EXACTLY WHAT IS ON THE EXAM.

For the best results, take this Practice Test as if it were the real exam. Set aside time when you will not be disturbed, and a location that is quiet and free of distractions. Read the instructions carefully, read each question carefully, and answer to the best of your ability.

Use the bubble answer sheets provided. When you have completed the Practice Test, check your answer against the Answer Key and read the explanation provided.

Practice Test Questions 2

Corrections Situational Judgement

Access 40 Corrections situational judgement questions in the Canada Corrections format online

https://courses.test-preparation.ca/course/sjt

Use Coupon - Sit-Judgement

Includes over 100 BONUS vocabulary question and How to Take a Test tutorial

Sentence Order

	A	B	C	D
1	○	○	○	○
2	○	○	○	○
3	○	○	○	○
4	○	○	○	○
5	○	○	○	○
6	○	○	○	○
7	○	○	○	○
8	○	○	○	○
9	○	○	○	○
10	○	○	○	○
11	○	○	○	○
12	○	○	○	○
13	○	○	○	○
14	○	○	○	○
15	○	○	○	○
16	○	○	○	○
17	○	○	○	○
18	○	○	○	○
19	○	○	○	○
20	○	○	○	○

Practice Test Questions 2
Reading and Sentence Correction

	A	B	C	D
1	○	○	○	○
2	○	○	○	○
3	○	○	○	○
4	○	○	○	○
5	○	○	○	○
6	○	○	○	○
7	○	○	○	○
8	○	○	○	○
9	○	○	○	○
10	○	○	○	○
11	○	○	○	○
12	○	○	○	○
13	○	○	○	○
14	○	○	○	○
15	○	○	○	○
16	○	○	○	○
17	○	○	○	○
18	○	○	○	○
19	○	○	○	○
20	○	○	○	○

Vocabulary

	A	B	C	D
1	○	○	○	○
2	○	○	○	○
3	○	○	○	○
4	○	○	○	○
5	○	○	○	○
6	○	○	○	○
7	○	○	○	○
8	○	○	○	○
9	○	○	○	○
10	○	○	○	○
11	○	○	○	○
12	○	○	○	○
13	○	○	○	○
14	○	○	○	○
15	○	○	○	○
16	○	○	○	○
17	○	○	○	○
18	○	○	○	○
19	○	○	○	○
20	○	○	○	○

Practice Test Questions 2

English Grammar

	A	B	C	D	E		A	B	C	D	E
1	○	○	○	○	○	21	○	○	○	○	○
2	○	○	○	○	○	22	○	○	○	○	○
3	○	○	○	○	○	23	○	○	○	○	○
4	○	○	○	○	○	24	○	○	○	○	○
5	○	○	○	○	○	25	○	○	○	○	○
6	○	○	○	○	○	26	○	○	○	○	○
7	○	○	○	○	○	27	○	○	○	○	○
8	○	○	○	○	○	28	○	○	○	○	○
9	○	○	○	○	○	29	○	○	○	○	○
10	○	○	○	○	○	30	○	○	○	○	○
11	○	○	○	○	○	31	○	○	○	○	○
12	○	○	○	○	○	32	○	○	○	○	○
13	○	○	○	○	○	33	○	○	○	○	○
14	○	○	○	○	○	34	○	○	○	○	○
15	○	○	○	○	○	35	○	○	○	○	○
16	○	○	○	○	○	36	○	○	○	○	○
17	○	○	○	○	○	37	○	○	○	○	○
18	○	○	○	○	○	38	○	○	○	○	○
19	○	○	○	○	○	39	○	○	○	○	○
20	○	○	○	○	○	40	○	○	○	○	○

Sentence Order

1.

A. However, if the mother's genes prevail, she will try to preserve herself for any future children.

B. This has led to a conflict between their genes.

C. In mammals, mothers are the primary caregivers, while males are rarely involved in the care of the offspring.

D. If the father's genes prevail, there is increased maternal care and investment.

   a. DACB
   b. CBAD
   c. CBDA
   d. DABC

2.

A. In fact, this is a current issue even for the US, where the maternal mortality ratio has risen in recent years.

B. Instead, many women give birth at home without any doctors, nurses, or trained midwives nearby.

C. However, many pregnant women do indeed die in developing countries because many of them can neither afford nor access medical help.

D. Researchers and public health workers are working hard to improve this dangerous situation for expecting mothers.

E. If you think that maternal mortality is mainly a problem in developing countries with poor medical care, you are far from the truth.

Practice Test Questions 2

    a. EACBD
    b. DEABC
    c. ECBAD
    d. CBDEA

3.

A. Consequently, children are often strongly aware of their gender and have clear ideas of different ways that girls and boys "should" look, act, and play.

B. Parents talk and play with their children every day, and we know that these interactions can have effects that last a lifetime.

C. Even though parents aren't always aware that they treat their sons and daughters differently, research has shown that many parents uphold gender stereotypes with their kids.

D. Depending on the child's gender, these interactions can be very different: girls and boys are often treated differently from a very young age.

    a. CBDA
    b. DBCA
    c. BCDA
    d. BDEA

4.

A. The reason for this is the lack of genetic diversity in commercial bananas, as all of these bananas are clones.

B. Farmers can protect their crops by applying chemicals that kill fungi, but this raises production costs and is bad for the environment.

C. So, any disease that can kill one of them can kill them all.

D. A fungal disease called Black Sigatoka threatens banana crops worldwide.

    a. CADB
    b. BDAC
    c. DACB
    d. DCAB

5.

A. The rainforest has many vital functions as it is home to a wide variety of different plants and animals.

B. If the Amazon Rainforest were a country, it would be the 9th biggest in the world.

C. This slows down global climate change and is another reason why it is so important to preserve our rainforests.

D. It also acts as a significant carbon sink by sucking it up from the atmosphere and storing it in plants and soil.

    a. BADB
    b. BDAC
    c. ABDC
    d. ADCA

Practice Test Questions 2

6.

A. For example, the fossil fuels burned to run tractors and harvesters, the gases released when cow manure decomposes, and when cows burp and fart.

B. Producing the foods we eat has massive environmental impacts: it requires vast tracts of land and vast quantities of water.

C. These emissions add up: scientists estimate that food production around the world causes up to 30% of all the greenhouse gases people release to the atmosphere each year.

D. In addition to using land and water, food production results in greenhouse gas emissions.

   a. CBDA
   b. BADC
   c. BDAC
   d. DBAC

7.

A. In 2012, DNA revealed that polar bears had faced extinction once before.

B. Polar bears have been struggling in the warming Arctic.

C. It likely happened during a warm period 130,000 years ago.

D. Afterward, the bears rebounded.

E. Though it's not the first time, the iconic species has suffered this fate.

   a. ABECD
   b. AECBD
   c. BAECD
   d. BEACD

8.

A. But a new type of glitter could change that.

B. Glitter and shimmery pigments are often made using toxic compounds or microplastics.

C. Such plant-based glitter could make arts and crafts more eco-friendly.

D. The new glitter is non-toxic and biodegradable as It is made using cellulose, which is found in plants.

    a. DCVA
    b. BADC
    c. BDCA
    d. CDBA

9.

A. That galaxy is some 28 million light-years from Earth.

B. The potential new world orbits two stars in the Whirlpool galaxy.

C. But until now, all of them have been inside our Milky Way galaxy.

D. Astronomers are calling the possible exoplanet M51-ULS-1b.

E. More than 4,800 planets have been discovered orbiting stars other than our sun.

    a. BAECD
    b. EBADA
    c. DEBAD
    d. ECBAD

Practice Test Questions 2

10.

A. Electricity is the term we use to describe the energy of charged particles.

B. When you connect a battery to a light bulb, electricity flows.

C. That is why electricity is also described as the flow of electrons between neighboring atoms.

D. This happens because electrical charges are free to carry energy from the battery through the bulb.

E. Electricity might be stored, like in a battery.

    a. BDCAE
    b. EBACD
    c. AEBCD
    d. AEBDC

11.

A. Others peer at distant words for evidence of life.

B. Some use telescopes to listen for messages broadcast by alien civilizations.

C. Alien-seeking researchers don't chase down UFOs, though.

D. Hunting for aliens might sound like science fiction, but it's serious science.

    a. DCAB
    b. BACD
    c. DCBA
    d. CBAD

12.

A. A former employee says Facebook chose to pursue profits even when it knew some people could be hurt by what was being posted on its apps.

B. You might be using Instagram or WhatsApp to stay in touch with friends.

C. Or, maybe you use them as entertainment.

D. However, for their owner Meta, these social media apps are a business that brings in lots of money.

    a. BDCA
    b. BCDA
    c. ABCD
    d. DBCA

13.

A. And even the most mythical ones often have closer ties to reality than you might think.

B. Halloween is a holiday about make-believe.

C. But not all Halloween creatures are fictional.

D. It's a night for telling ghost stories and dressing up as witches and werewolves.

    a. CADB
    b. DCBA
    c. BCDA
    d. BDCA

Practice Test Questions 2

14.

A. The hits causing changes do not even have to be hard enough to cause a concussion, a type of traumatic brain injury.

B. A new study finds that young players' heads can get hit hundreds of times each season.

C. American football is a rough game, even at the middle-school level.

D. Those hits can leave their mark on a young player's brain.

    a. CDBA
    b. BADC
    c. CBDA
    d. ADCB

15.

A. Some later undergo surgery.

B. It involves letting young kids use a name and pronouns that match their gender.

C. The term gender-affirming health care includes treatments that help people express their gender identity.

D. This care looks different for people of different ages.

E. Adolescents may take drugs to delay puberty, followed by hormones.

    a. EABDC
    b. EBDCA
    c. CBCDA
    d. CDBEA

16.

A. It's easy to think that only people who vape regularly face any health risks.

B. Last year, nearly one in three high schoolers used e-cigarettes daily or almost daily.

C. Vaped nicotine is now one of the most common drugs used by U.S. teens.

D. Moreover, it causes the type of damage that underlies many long-term diseases.

E. However, a new study finds that a single vape session damages cells.

    a. AEDCB
    b. CAEDB
    c. CBAED
    d. BCADE

17.

A. Additionally, critical thinking should not be confused with being argumentative or being critical of other people.

B. Critical thinking is not a matter of accumulating information.

C. Instead, a critical thinker should be able to deduce consequences from what he knows and should be able to make use of information to solve problems and seek relevant sources of information to inform himself.

D. For example, a person with good memory and who knows a lot of facts is not necessarily good at critical thinking.

    a. BACD
    b. BCDA
    c. CBAD
    d. BDCA

Practice Test Questions 2

18.

A. Specifically, through the motifs of storytelling and weaving, the epics illustrated ideal femininity through Penelope and unideal femininity through Helen.

B. Literature tends to reflect the values of the era in which it was written, and this Ancient Greek poem is no exception.

C. However, Helen and Penelope's female characters stand out against this male backdrop.

D. It is no surprise that the Homeric epics are focused almost entirely on the woes and triumphs of men.

   a. DBCA
   b. BDCA
   c. DCAB
   d. BDAC

19.

A. Penelope, in contrast, utilized storytelling to build upon male dominance.

B. The Homeric poets utilized storytelling and the loom to represent ideal versus unideal femininity.

C. Her stories were mixed with references to Odysseus, laced with her yearning for him, and spiked with her loyalty to him.

D. Primarily, the character of Helen used the art of storytelling to practice agency and defy the male narrative in the Odyssey.

   a. ACDB
   b. DCAB
   c. BDCA
   d. BDAC

20.

A. In literary and cinematic traditions, this romantic nature of female suicides has been used as a trope to represent an act of agency and empowerment during which the female chooses death over conforming to societal injustices.

B. In both examples, the female body is overtly sexualized, portraying suicide as a romantic death.

C. However, it is imperative to re-examine these revered works not through a traditional critical lens but through an ethical lens.

D. The Virgin Suicides, written by Jeffrey Eugenides and Sofia Coppola's film adaptation, utilize the literary and cinematic tropes of suicide to explore female suicides as romantic notions.

    a. DBAC
    b. ACDB
    c. DABC
    d. ABCD

READING

Directions: The following questions are based on several reading passages. A series of questions follow each passage. Read each passage carefully, and then answer the questions based on it. You may reread the passage as often as you wish. When you have finished answering the questions based on one passage, go right onto the next passage. Choose the best answer based on the information given and implied.

PRACTICE TEST QUESTIONS 2

Questions 1 and 2 refer to the following passage.

Women and Advertising

Only in the last few generations have media messages been so widespread and so readily seen, heard, and read by so many people. Advertising is an important part of both selling and buying anything from soap to cereal to jeans. For whatever reason, more consumers are women than are men. Media message are subtle but powerful, and more attention has been paid lately to how these message affect women.
Of all the products that women buy, makeup, clothes, and other stylistic or cosmetic products are among the most popular. This means that companies focus their advertising on women, promising them that their product will make her feel, look, or smell better than the next company's product will. This competition has resulted in advertising that is more and more ideal and less and less possible for everyday women. However, because women do look to these ideals and the products they represent as how they can potentially become, many women have developed unhealthy attitudes about themselves when they have failed to become those ideals.
In recent years, more companies have tried to change advertisements to be healthier for women. This includes featuring models of more sizes and addressing a huge outcry against unfair tools such as airbrushing and photo editing. There is debate about what the right balance between real and ideal is, because fashion is also considered art and some changes are made to purposefully elevate fashionable products and signify that they are creative, innovative, and the work of individual people. Artists want their freedom protected as much as women do, and advertising agencies are often caught in the middle.

Some claim that the companies who make these changes are not doing enough. Many people worry that there are still not enough models of different sizes and different ethnicities. Some people claim that companies use this healthier type of advertisement not for the good of women, but because they would like to sell products to the women who are looking for these kinds of messages. This is also a hard balance to find:

companies do need to make money, and women do need to feel respected.

While the focus of this change has been on women, advertising can also affect men, and this change will hopefully be a lesson on media for all consumers.

1. The second paragraph states that advertising focuses on women

    a. to shape what the ideal should be

    b. because women buy makeup

    c. because women are easily persuaded

    d. because of the types of products that women buy

2. The author uses the phrase "for whatever reason" in this passage to

    a. keep the focus of the paragraph on media messages and not on the differences between men and women

    b. show that the reason for this is unimportant

    c. argue that it is stupid that more women are consumers than men

    d. show that he or she is tired of talking about why media messages are important

Question 3 refers to the following passage.

FDR, the Treaty of Versailles, and the Fourteen Points

At the conclusion of World War I, those who had won the war and those who were forced to admit defeat welcomed the end of the war and expected that a peace treaty would be signed. The American president, Franklin D. Roosevelt, played an important part in proposing what the agreements should be and did so through his Fourteen Points.
World War I had begun in 1914 when an Austrian archduke was assassinated, leading to a domino effect that pulled the

world's most powerful countries into war on a large scale. The war catalyzed the creation and use of deadly weapons that had not previously existed, resulting in a great loss of soldiers on both sides of the fighting. More than 9 million soldiers were killed.

The United States agreed to enter the war right before it ended, and many believed that its decision to become finally involved brought on the end of the war. FDR made it very clear that the U.S. was entering the war for moral reasons and had an agenda focused on world peace. The Fourteen Points were individual goals and ideas (focused on peace, free trade, open communication, and self reliance) that FDR wanted the power nations to strive for now that the war had concluded. He was optimistic and had many ideas about what could be accomplished through and during the post-war peace. However, FDR's fourteen points were poorly received when he presented them to the leaders of other world powers, many of whom wanted only to help their own countries and to punish the Germans for fuelling the war, and they fell by the wayside. World War II was imminent, for Germany lost everything.

Some historians believe that the other leaders who participated in the Treaty of Versailles weren't receptive to the Fourteen Points because World War I was fought almost entirely on European soil, and the United States lost much less than did the other powers. FDR was in a unique position to determine the fate of the war, but doing it on his own terms did not help accomplish his goals. This is only one historical example of how the United State has tried to use its power as an important country, but found itself limited because of geological or ideological factors.

3. The main idea of this passage is that

    a. World War I was unfair because no fighting took place in America

    b. World War II happened because of the Treaty of Versailles

    c. the power the United States has to help other countries also prevents it from helping other countries

    d. Franklin D. Roosevelt was one of the United States' smartest presidents.

Correcting Sentences

Abuse of Science: The Atom Bomb

Questions 4 - 7 refer to the following passage

The cost of the two World Wars – not to mention the lives lost – could have easily paid for the entire energy consumption of the nations which waged them. [1] Even today, world powers are spending hundreds of billions of dollars sponsoring wars in a bid to control oil-rich areas. [2] Spending such astronomic sums on peaceful, environment friendly sources of energy would certainly produce results that would limit the energy needs of the planet as a whole. [3] Not to mention, resolving the conflicts between warring nations. [4]

For instance the atom bomb was developed during the Second World War by the recommendations of the great Albert Einstein - who is accepted as the father of modern physics; in fear of the Germans developing it and using on the Allies. [5] No matter what, the technology behind the atom bomb essentially had the power to resolve the war. [6] Using it to produce energy for power was an option wide open to be explored by scientists. [7] Today, as many as forty countries including countries like Egypt, harness nuclear energy as a dominant source of power alongside mainstream carbon sources. [8]

The two atom bombs dropped at Hiroshima and Nagasaki, as the consequence of the tragedy at Pearl Harbor, left catastrophic legacies to the generations that followed. [9] The generations that followed still have not recovered from the genetic disorders. [10] Almost seven decades passing later, abnormal births and birth defects continue to occur. [11]

Practice Test Questions 2

4. Which sentence from the passage is an example of a sentence fragment?

    a. 3

    b. 4

    c. 5

    d. 6

5. Which of the following changes would focus attention on the main idea of the second paragraph?

    a. Yet, the technology behind the atom bomb essentially had the power of resolving the war itself which scientists like him failed to convey.

    b. As a result of that, the technology behind the atom bomb essentially had the power of resolving the war itself which scientists like him failed to convey.

    c. With respect to that, the technology behind the atom bomb essentially had the power of resolving the war itself which scientists like him failed to convey.

    d. Additionally, the technology behind the atom bomb essentially had the power of resolving the war itself which scientists like him failed to convey.

6. Which of the following changes are needed in sentence 5?

    a. For instance the atom bomb was developed during the Second World War by the recommendations of the great Albert Einstein - who is accepted as the father of modern physics - in fear of the Germans developing it and using on the Allies.

    b. For instance, the atom bomb was developed during the Second World War by the recommendations of the great Albert Einstein - who is accepted as the father of modern physics - in fear of the Germans developing it and using on the Allies.

    c. For instance, the atom bomb was developed during the Second World War by the recommendations of the great Albert Einstein; who is accepted as the father of modern physics - in fear of the Germans developing it and using on the Allies.

d. For instance, the atom bomb was developed during the Second World War by the recommendations of the great Albert Einstein; who is accepted as the father of modern physics, in fear of the Germans developing it and using on the Allies.

7. Which of the following sentences, if inserted before sentence 7, would best illustrate the main idea of the passage?

a. The name of the technology is widely referred to in current science books published worldwide as nuclear fission.

b. This technology is, however, misused by many irresponsible states in the world today.

c. Nuclear fission that is used in the fuelling of the bomb, has the capacity to produce electrical energy which has turned out to be a major alternative later in the Twentieth Century.

d. Nuclear fission, which is the main technology behind the development of the atom bomb can also be used to produce gamma rays which has many applications in medical science.

Leg Surgery

Questions 8 - 11 refer to the following passage

The main reason many young women opt for surgery, despite the pain, inconvenience and cost, is the height discrimination in an increasingly competitive job market. [1] Almost all firms put certain height criteria for the candidates who apply. [2] For example, for an air stewardess position, women must be no more than 163 cm tall; whereas for jobs in foreign affairs, Chinese diplomats are required to match their foreign counterparts. [3] Height concerns also effect routine citizenship privileges such as driving licenses, which require a height of at least 157 cm to be eligible for taking the test in some places. [4]

The urge to undergo surgery is becoming increasingly popular among Chinese males as well. [5] "It offers me a 10 cm increase in my height, which can dramatically change my future," says Jing Yong, an interpreter working in Hong Kong. [6] "This will allow me better opportunities in the competitive job market here," adds the young multilingual who couldn't make it to the foreign ministry for being below 168 cm. [7] Even parents approve of the idea, being fully aware of all the complexity and they are willing to finance such a labyrinth surgery. [8] "It's something that will give her confidence and achieve her goals in life. [9] Her height used to bother her tremendously, now this can change that," comments Swee Jing's father by her bedside as she is recovering from the eighteen-months process that involves elongating her tibia and fibula by placing two rods that will stimulate the extra growth of the bones. [10] They too are hopeful about the possibilities the surgery would affect the life of their daughter. [11]

8. Which sentence in the second paragraph is least relevant to the main idea of the first paragraph?

    a. 2
    b. 3
    c. 4
    d. 5

9. Which sentence is not consistent with the author's purpose?

    a. 3
    b. 6
    c. 9
    d. 12

10. Which of the following sentences, if inserted after sentence 7, would best illustrate the main idea of the passage?

    a. This is the main reason I am willing to undergo this surgery

    b. This artificial way of gaining height is turning out to be a new trend among the new generation in height conscious China.

    c. Height is a very big problem for Chinese people, particularly for those who wish to go abroad and carry the flag of China there.

    d. Young people like Yong will have to spend the rest of their lives with a fake pair of legs though.

11. Which of the following changes are needed in sentence 8?

    a. Even parents approve of the idea, being fully aware of all the sophistications and they are willing to finance such a labyrinth surgery.

    b. Even parents approve of the idea, being fully aware of all the complications and they are willing to finance such a sophisticated surgery.

    c. Even parents approve of the idea, being fully aware of all the complexity and they are willing to finance such a sophisticated surgery.

    d. Even parents approve of the idea, being fully aware of all the complexity and they are willing to finance such a sophisticated surgery.

My Friend Luke

Questions 12 - 15 refer to the following passage

My forty-year old friend Luke is possibly the sweetest, shyest person enjoying his life on the entire Earth. [1] He is somewhat short, skinny and upright; has a thin moustache and a thinner trace of hair covering his head. [2] And since he has problems seeing distant things, he wears glasses that are small, thick and frameless; the round coffee-brown colored glasses give him a cool appearance uniquely suited to his personality. [3] Which I doubt belongs to any other person. [4]

There are traits in him seldom found in others. [5] While in a crowd, he walks sideways so as not to trouble others. [6] Instead of requesting a space to move ahead, he glides past to one side of the person blocking in his way. [7] If the gap turns out to be so narrow that it does not permit his bony frame to pass, he waits patiently for the person to move out of the way. [8] He is panicked by street dogs and neighbors' cats and to avoid them, he crosses to the other side of the street every now and then. [9]

Luke never speaks, as he thinks speaking is a waste of energy; something he is vehemently dedicated to saving. [10] Whenever he does, in order not to interrupt anybody, he speaks with a very soft, low tone – in a way no one ever notices him speaking in the first place. [11] Quite ironically, when he gets a rare chance to speak, he never succeeds in speaking more than two words before being interrupted by others. [12]

12. What sentence from the passage is an example of a sentence fragment?

    a. 4
    b. 5
    c. 6
    d. 7

13. Which sentence in the second paragraph is least relevant to the main idea of the second paragraph?

    a. 6
    b. 7
    c. 8
    d. 9

14. Which of the following sentences should be modified to reduce redundancy?

    a. 2
    b. 3
    c. 4
    d. 5

15. Which of the following sentences, if inserted before sentence 1, would best illustrate the main idea of the passage?

    a. But that does not bother him; rather he always seems to be happy in being able to utter those two words.

    b. Interestingly, he never insists in speaking with people more eloquently.

    c. What is more ironic, he never worked on his social skills and diction to be more communicative.

    d. As a result, Luke feels like hitting those interrupting him in their face.

Of Ease and Discipline

Questions 16 - 19 refer to the following passage

Looking at his watch, Ray thought it was time for a break. [1] So, he let the kids wrap their things up and head out of the classroom. [2] They seemed to like the idea of an extra five minutes before they would start with the boring recitation, turning page after page as one of them stood and read through the old Shakespearean dialect. [3] Some were interested in chatting with him as they approached him with the usual curiosity about a new teacher joining their class. [4] What they didn't know was he was their new music teacher just replacing the dull Mr. Drodsky who happened to be an 'expert' in American Literature with his dreadful Eastern European accent. [5] But for a day only. [6]

Practice Test Questions 2

They were excited about the rhetoric that they finally have been spared of Mr. Drodsky's shrieking inquiries of "Aa you wiss me, chilsren?" [7] But as they came to know him closely, they were disappointed he would only occupy Mr. Drodsky's position for two weeks. [8] Mr. Drodsky was ill and would be away for the next fifteen days. [9] They seemed to like the news, but were also reluctant to be happy about it. [10] Nevertheless, they were happy about the substitution today and the arrival of their new music teacher. [11] The school would return to their jolly old days with regular music lessons and the parties. [12]

With ring of the bell, all the boys and girls started filling their seats as Ray continued chatting with the ones who had asked him about himself. [13] In a moment all the students – out of their old habits – were ready with their books open, waiting for the teacher to dictate who was in queue to read. [14] Ray was somewhat perplexed as he found this obedience unusual, especially in this century. [15] Coming from a public school in New Jersey, Ray had never seen students 'tamed' to such narrow, desperate discipline in his six years of experience as a music teacher. [16]

16. What sentence from the passage is an example of a sentence fragment?

    a. 3
    b. 4
    c. 5
    d. 6

17. Which sentence is not consistent with the author's purpose?

    a. 6
    b. 7
    c. 9
    d. 10

18. Which of the following changes are needed in sentence 16?

a. Coming from a public school in New Jersey, Ray had never seen students 'tamed' to such narrow, disparate discipline in his six years of experience as a music teacher.

b. Coming from a public school in New Jersey, Ray had never seen students 'tanned' to such narrow, disparate discipline in his six years of experience as a music teacher.

c. Coming from a public school in New Jersey, Ray had never seen students 'turned' to such narrow, desperate discipline in his six years of experience as a music teacher.

d. No change.

19. Which of the following sentences contains non-standard usage?

a. 4
b. 5
c. 6
d. 7

Spiderman

Question 20 refers to the following passage

Spiders have always fascinated Johnson. [1] Ever since his childhood visit to his grandfather's farm in Vancouver where he first saw them in a large web that almost covered the gate of the granary warehouse, he looked for spiders everywhere he visited. [2] He would search for spider webs even in the high rise apartments such as the one he lives in now. [3] He would find them there too. [4] Hanging between two walls near one corner of the store room, a magnificent piece of art left half woven and still being worked on. [5]

It is not the life of the spiders itself that attracted Johnson, rather their art. [6] He likes their delicate webs. [7] The amazing shape and sizes of the webs. [8] The symmetry, the balance, the intricate design and the detailed network fascinates him. [9] He wanders how they manage to create something unique like this with such a little brain that they have. [10] That is why he likes to catch them in action, while they are weaving. [11]

When he opened the store room this week, he saw the huge web in the left corner touching the roof. [12] That has been there for almost six months now and it lay there as it were last month. [13] No strands added. [14] It took on a grayish shade from the dust it gathered over the weeks, making it obvious that Binny has stopped working on it. [15] Hanging here and there in the web are some dry mosquitoes that were spared by the monster that owns the trap. [16]

In the far left, on the wall adjacent to the door, Johnson is trying to build a web out of string and glue -without much success! [17] "Incredible, you little genius!" Johnson murmurs to himself. [18]

20. What sentence from the passage is an example of a sentence fragment?

    a. 2
    b. 3
    c. 4
    d. 5

VOCABULARY

1. Choose the adjective that means shocking, terrible or wicked.

    a. Pleasantries
    b. Heinous
    c. Shrewd
    d. Provencal

2. Choose the noun that means a person of thing that tells or announces the coming of someone or something.

    a. Harbinger
    b. Evasion
    c. Bleak
    d. Craven

3. Choose a word that means the same as the underlined word.

He wasn't especially generous. All the servings were very judicious.

    a. Abundant
    b. Careful
    c. Sparing
    d. Careless

4. Because of the growing use of _____ as a fuel, corn production has greatly increased.

    a. Alcohol
    b. Ethanol
    c. Natural gas
    d. Oil

5. In heavily industrialized areas, the pollution of the air causes many to develop _____ diseases.

    a. Respiratory
    b. Cardiac
    c. Alimentary
    d. Circulatory

Practice Test Questions 2

6. Choose the best definition of inherent.

    a. To receive money in a will

    b. An essential part of

    c. To receive money from a will

    d. None of the above

7. Choose the best vapid.

    a. adj. tasteless or bland

    b. v. To inflict, as a revenge or punishment

    c. v. to convert into gas

    d. v. to go up in smoke

8. Choose the best definition of waif.

    a. n. a sick and hungry child

    b. n. an orphan staying in a foster home

    c. n. homeless child or stray

    d. n. a type of French bread eaten with cheese

9. Choose the adjective that means similar or identical.

    a. Soluble

    b. Assembly

    c. Conclave

    d. Homologous

10. Choose a word with the same meaning as the underlined word.

We used that operating system 20 years ago, now it is <u>obsolete</u>.

    a. Functional
    b. Disused
    c. Obese
    d. None of the Above

11. Choose the word with the same meaning as the underlined word

His bad manners really <u>rankle</u> me.

    a. Annoy
    b. Obsolete
    c. Enliven
    d. None of the above

12. Because hydroelectric power is a _____ source of energy, its use is excellent for the environment.

    a. Significant
    b. Disposable
    c. Renewable
    d. Reusable

13. Choose the best definition of torpid.

    a. Fast
    b. Rapid
    c. Sluggish
    d. Violent

Practice Test Questions 2

14. Choose the best definition of gregarious.

   a. Sociable
   b. Introverted
   c. Large
   d. Solitary

15. Choose the best definition of mutation.

   a. v. To utter with a loud and vehement voice
   b. n. change or alteration
   c. n. An act or exercise of will
   d. v. To cause to be one

16. Choose the best definition of lithe.

   a. adj. small in size
   b. adj. Artificial
   c. adj. flexible or plaint
   d. adj. fake

17. Choose the best definition of resent.

   a. adj. To express displeasure or indignation
   b. v. To cause to be one
   c. adj. Clumsy
   d. adj. strong feelings of love

18. Choose and adjective that means irrelevant or not having substance or matter

   a. Immaterial
   b. Prohibition
   c. Prediction
   d. Brokerage

19. Choose and adjective that means perfect, no faults or errors.

   a. Impeccable
   b. Formidable
   c. Genteel
   d. Disputation

20. Choose the best definition of pudgy.

   a. v. to draw general inferences
   b. Adj. fat, plump and overweight
   c. n. permanence
   d. adj. spoilt or bad condition

English Grammar, Punctuation, Capitalization and Usage.

1. Jessica's father was in the Navy, so she attended schools in Newark; New Jersey, Key West; Florida, San Diego, California, and Fairbanks, Alaska.

   a. Jessica's father was in the Navy, so she attended schools in Newark, New Jersey, Key West, Florida, San Diego, California, and Fairbanks, Alaska.
   b. Jessica's father was in the Navy, so she attended schools in: Newark, New Jersey, Key West, Florida, San Diego, California, and Fairbanks, Alaska.
   c. Jessica's father was in the Navy, so she attended schools in Newark, New Jersey; Key West, Florida; San Diego, California; and Fairbanks, Alaska.
   d. None of the choices are correct.

Practice Test Questions 2

2. George wrecked John's <u>car; that</u> was the end of their friendship.

    a. George wrecked John's car that was the end of their friendship.

    b. George wrecked John's car. that was the end of their friendship.

    c. The sentence is correct.

    d. None of the choices are correct.

3. The dress was not Gina's <u>favorite, however,</u> she wore it to the dance.

    a. The dress was not Gina's favorite; however, she wore it to the dance.

    b. None of the choices are correct.

    c. The dress was not Gina's favorite, however; she wore it to the dance.

    d. The dress was not Gina's favorite however, she wore it to the dance.

4. Chris showed his dedication to golf in many <u>ways; for</u> example, he watched all the tournaments on television.

    a. Chris showed his dedication to golf in many ways, for example, he watched all the tournaments on television.

    b. The sentence is correct.

    c. Chris showed his dedication to golf in many ways, for example; he watched all the tournaments on television.

    d. Chris showed his dedication to golf in many ways for example he watched all the tournaments on television.

5. There was scarcely <u>no food</u> in the pantry, because <u>not nobody</u> ate at home.

a. There was scarcely no food in the pantry, because nobody ate at home.

b. There was scarcely any food in the pantry, because nobody ate at home.

c. There was scarcely any food in the pantry, because not nobody ate at home.

d. The sentence is correct.

6. Choose the sentence with the correct grammar.

a. If Joe had told me the truth, I wouldn't have been so angry.

b. If Joe would have told me the truth, I wouldn't have been so angry.

c. I wouldn't have been so angry if Joe would have told the truth.

d. If Joe would have telled me the truth, I wouldn't have been so angry.

7. Michael <u>have lived</u> in that house for forty years, while I <u>has owned</u> this one for only six weeks.

a. Michael has lived in that house for forty years, while I has owned this one for only six weeks.

b. Michael have lived in that house for forty years, while I have owned this one for only six weeks.

c. None of the choices are correct.

d. Michael has lived in that house for forty years, while I have owned this one for only six weeks.

PRACTICE TEST QUESTIONS 2

8. Until you <u>take</u> the overdue books to the library, you can't <u>take</u> any new ones home.

    a. Until you take the overdue books to the library, you can't take any new ones home
    b. Until you take the overdue books to the library, you can't bring any new ones home.
    c. Until you bring the overdue books to the library, you can't take any new ones home.
    d. None of the choices are correct.

9. If they had <u>gone</u> to the party, he would have <u>gone</u> too.

    a. The sentence is correct.

    b. If they had went to the party, he would have gone too.

    c. If they had gone to the party, he would have went too.

    d. If they had went to the party, he would have went too.

10. His doctor suggested that he eat <u>fewer</u> snacks and do <u>fewer</u> lounging on the couch.

    a. His doctor suggested that he eat less snacks and do fewer lounging on the couch.

    b. His doctor suggested that he eat fewer snacks and do less lounging on the couch.

    c. His doctor suggested that he eat less snacks and do less lounging on the couch.

    d. None of the choices are correct.

11. Lee pronounced <u>it's</u> name incorrectly; <u>it's</u> an impa-tiens, not an impatience.

    a. The sentence is correct.

    b. Lee pronounced its name incorrectly; its an *impa-tiens*, not an *impatience*.

    c. Lee pronounced it's name incorrectly; its an *impa-tiens*, not an *impatience*.

    d. Lee pronounced its name incorrectly; it's an *impa-tiens*, not an *impatience*.

12. There <u>was, however</u> very little difference between the two.

    a. There was however, very little difference between the two.

    b. None of the choices are correct.

    c. There was; however, very little difference between the two.

    d. There was, however, very little difference between the two.

13. The Ford Motor Company was named for Henry Ford

    a. which had founded the company.

    b. who founded the company.

    c. whose had founded the company.

    d. whom had founded the company.

14. Thomas Edison _____ after he invented the light bulb, television, motion pictures, and phonograph.

    a. has always been known as the greatest inventor

    b. was always been known as the greatest inventor

    c. must have had been always known as the greatest inventor

    d. will had been known as the greatest inventor

Practice Test Questions 2

15. The weatherman on Channel 6 said that this has been the _____.

    a. most hottest summer on record.

    b. hottest summer on record.

    c. hotter summer on record.

    d. None of the above

16. Although Joe is tall for his age, his brother Elliot is _____ of the two.

    a. the tallest

    b. more tallest

    c. the tall

    d. the taller

17. I can never remember how to use those two common words, "sell," meaning to trade a product for money, or _____ meaning an event where products are traded for less money than usual.

    a. sale-

    b. "sale,"

    c. "sale

    d. "to sale,"

18. His father is

    a. a poet and novelist

    b. poet and novelist

    c. a poet and a novelist

    d. none of the above

19. The class just finished reading , _____ a short story by Carl Stephenson about a plantation owner's battle with army ants.

    a. -"Leinengen versus the Ants,"

    b. Leinengen versus the Ants,

    c. "Leinengen versus the Ants,"

    d. Leinengen versus the Ants

20. After the car was fixed it _____ again.

    a. ran good

    b. ran well

    c. would have run well

    d. ran more well

21. "Where does the sun go during the _____ asked little Kathy.

    a. night,"

    b. night?",

    c. night,?"

    d. night?"

22. Vegetables are a <u>healthy</u> food; eating them can make you more <u>healthy</u>.

    a. Vegetables are a healthy food; eating them can make you more healthful.

    b. Vegetables are a healthful food; eating them can make you more healthful.

    c. None of the choices are correct.

    d. Vegetables are a healthful food; eating them can make you more healthy.

PRACTICE TEST QUESTIONS 2

23. When James went <u>in</u> his room, he found that his clothes had been put <u>in</u> the closet.

   a. When James went into his room, he found that his clothes had been put in the closet.

   b. None of the choices are correct.

   c. When James went into his room, he found that his clothes had been put into the closet.

   d. When James went in his room, he found that his clothes had been put into the closet.

24. After you lay the books on the counter, you may lay down for a nap.

   a. The sentence is correct.

   b. After you lie the books on the counter, you may lay down for a nap.

   c. After you lay the books on the counter, you may lie down for a nap.

   d. After you lay the books on the counter, you may lay down for a nap.

25. Don <u>would never of thought</u> of that book, but you <u>could have reminded</u> him.

   a. Don would never have thought of that book, but you could have reminded him.

   b. None of the choices are correct.

   c. Don would never have thought of that book, but you could of have reminded him.

   d. Don would never of thought of that book, but you could of reminded him.

26. Mrs. Foster <u>learned</u> me many things, but I was <u>taught</u> the most by Mr. Wallace.

   a. Mrs. Foster taught me many things, but I learned the most from Mr. Wallace.

   b. The sentence is correct.

   c. Mrs. Foster learned me many things, but I learned the most from Mr. Wallace.

   d. None of the choices are correct.

27. He did not have to <u>loose</u> the race; if only his shoes weren't so <u>loose</u>!

   a. He did not have to loose the race; if only his shoes weren't so lose!

   b. He did not have to lose the race; if only his shoes weren't so loose!

   c. The sentence is correct.

   d. None of the choices are correct.

28. The attorney did not want to <u>prosecute</u> the defendant; his goal was to <u>prosecute</u> the guilty party.

   a. None of the choices are correct.

   b. The attorney did not want to persecute the defendant; his goal was to persecute the guilty party.

   c. The attorney did not want to prosecute the defendant; his goal was to persecute the guilty party.

   d. The attorney did not want to persecute the defendant; his goal was to prosecute the guilty party.

Practice Test Questions 2

29. The speeches must <u>proceed</u> the election; the election cannot <u>proceed</u> without hearing from the candidates.

    a. The speeches must precede the election; the election cannot proceed without hearing from the candidates.

    b. The speeches must precede the election; the election cannot precede without hearing from the candidates.

    c. The speeches must proceed the election; the election cannot precede without hearing from the candidates.

    d. The sentence is correct.

30. My best friend said, "Always Count your Change."

    a. My best friend said, "always count your change."

    b. The sentence is correct.

    c. My best friend said, "Always count your change."

    d. None of the choices are correct.

31. The <u>Victorian Era</u> was in the <u>nineteenth century</u>.

    a. The sentence is correct.

    b. The victorian era was in the nineteenth century.

    c. The Victorian Era was in the Nineteenth century.

    d. The Victorian era was in the Nineteenth century.

32. I prefer <u>pepsi</u> to <u>Coke</u>.

    a. I prefer pepsi to coke.

    b. The sentence is correct.

    c. I prefer Pepsi to Coke.

    d. None of the choices are correct.

33. I always have **french fries** with my **coke**.

    a. The sentence is correct.

    b. I always have french fries with my Coke.

    c. I always have French Fries with my Coke.

    d. None of the choices are correct.

34. The **blue Jays** are my favorite team.

    a. The blue jays are my favorite team.

    b. The sentence is correct.

    c. The Blue Jays are my favorite team.

    d. None of the choices are correct.

35. The **Southwest** is the best part of the country.

    a. The sentence is correct.

    b. The southwest is the best part of the country.

    c. The southwest is the best part of the Country.

    d. None of the choices are correct.

Practice Test Questions 2

Answer Key

Sentence Order

1. C
The opening sentence is C as it introduces the topic, and all the other sentences contain transition words. The comes B as it develops the topic and then D and E explain how the conflict of the genes works.

2. A
The first sentence is E, and it starts the sequence with the clause. Then comes A, as it illustrates that maternal mortality is a problem in the US as well. Then comes C that contradicts the previous sentence. Then B as it explains the situation in developing countries. Lastly, D demonstrates that this situation is being taken care of.

3. D
The first sentence can either be B or C. However, B contains more general information than C, so it's the opening one, and then it's followed by C. As A contains the word 'consequently,' it should be the last one. So, after C comes D and then the E and A.

4. C
The opening sentence is D as it brings up information about fungal disease - Black Sigatoka. Then comes A, followed by C, as they specify why this disease is dangerous for the banana crops worldwide. The last sentence is B, as it shows that there is a way to protect bananas and shows its side effects as well.

5. A

The first sentence can be either B or However, B won't make any logical sense in any other place as it is a clause that mentions the Amazon Rainforest for the first time. So B is followed by Then comes D, and it adds information on what Rainforest does, and lastly, C gives a conclusion.

6. C

The sequence starts with B as it opens the topic. Then comes D, as it adds to the information provided in B. A gives an example for the greenhouse gas emissions mentioned in D, and lastly, C summarizes the sequence.

7. D

The opening sentence is B, as it is about the current issue of polar bears. Then comes E as 'this fate' refers to the issue stated in B. A follows this and gives the information that this issue has happened in the past. C specifies when and lastly, D.

8. B

The first sentence can be either B or D. However, D is about a new type of glitter, and considering other sentences, the sequence should start with B. Then we will have A, and that will be followed by D. Lastly, C will give a conclusive sentence.

9. D

The first sentence is E, as it gives the opening general information. Then comes C, as it states that all of these planets were discovered in our galaxy. Following one is B as it proceeds the information about the new discovery, then A and D as they add more details. A follows B as 'that galaxy' refers to the Whirlpool galaxy.

10. C

The openings sentence is A as it gives the description of electricity. From the other sentences, E should be prior to B as it connected the electricity to the battery. D should follow B as it explains that electricity is a flow and C is the continuation of D.

11. C

The first sentence is D, as all the others contain transition words. Then comes C, 'though' at the ends shows that it's a contradiction to the first sentence. Following one is B and then A.

Practice Test Questions 2

12. B

The first sentence in the sequence should be B as it starts the topic. Then comes C, as it is the continuation of the first sentence. The following will be D, which contains the connecting word and contradicts the prior information. And lastly, A is proof of the statement provided in D.

13. D

The first sentence is B as it opens the topic - Halloween. Then comes D, which develops the subject. C contradicts the information about Halloween being fictional, and lastly, A states that some Halloween stories are close to reality.

14. C

The first sentence is C, as it provides a general topic. Then comes B, which explains why the sport is dangerous. The following one is D specifies what kind of damage it can cause, and lastly, A adds the intensity to the information in D.

15. D

The opening sentence is C which the new term is introduced. Then comes D, which is then specified in B - what this term refers to for young people. Then E and A create one segment - what this term refers to for adults.

16. C

The first sentence is C as it opens the topic, and all the others contain transitional words. Then comes B, as it gives the statistics to prove the first statement. Then comes A, followed by E, which contradicts A, and D, which adds information about the damage vape can cause.

17. D

The first sentence should be B as it starts the topic, and all the others contain transitional words. The next one is D, as it gives an example that a person having a good memory doesn't mean he has critical thinking. Then C explains what critical thinking means in that sense, and lastly, A adds some details about critical thinking so it won't be confused with being critical.

18. A
The first sentence should be D as all the others contain transitional words suggesting that they are referring to the information prior. Then comes B as it generalizes the topic in D. The next one is C as it provides contradictory information about female characters. And the last one is A, which specifies this information.

19. D
The first sentence is B as it introduces the topic. Also, all the others contain transition words, meaning they refer to the prior information. The second one will be D, as it presents the first example for the topic. Then A is about Penelope, and it compares and contradicts her to Helen. Lastly, C, as it clearly is about Penelope as the loyalty for the man is mentioned.

20. A
The first sentence can either be D or C is a follow-up to A as it contains the contradictory connecting word -' however.' Similarly, B is a continuation of D as 'in both examples' refers to information in it. Logical will be to start the sequence with D as it presents the book and the movie, and then other sentences will widen this topic.

Reading and Sentence Correction

1. D
This question tests the reader's summarization skills. The other choices A, B, and C focus on portions of the second paragraph that are too narrow and do not relate to the specific portion of text in question. The complexity of the sentence may mislead students into selecting one of these answers, but rearranging or restating the sentence will lead the reader to the correct answer. In addition, choice A makes an assumption that may or may not be true about the intentions of the company, choice B focuses on one product rather than the idea of the products, and choice C makes an assumption about women that may or may not be true and is not supported by the text.

Practice Test Questions 2

2. A

This question tests reader's vocabulary and summarization skills. This phrase, used by the author, may seem flippant and dismissive if readers focus on the word "whatever" and misinterpret it as a popular, colloquial term. In this way, Choices B and C may mislead the reader to selecting one of them by including the terms "unimportant" and "stupid," respectively. Choice D is a similar misreading, but doesn't make sense when the phrase is at the beginning of the passage and the entire passage is on media messages. Choice A is literally and contextually appropriate, and the reader can understand that the author would like to keep the introduction focused on the topic the passage is going to discuss.

3. C

This question tests the reader's summarization skills. The entire passage is leading up to the idea that the president of the US may not have had grounds to assert his Fourteen Points when other countries had lost so much. Choice A is pretty directly inferred by the text, but it does not adequately summarize what the entire passage is trying to communicate. Choice B may also be inferred by the passage when it says that the war is "imminent," but it does not represent the entire message, either. The passage does seem to be in praise of FDR, or at least in respect of him, but it does not in any way claim that he is the smartest president, nor does this represent the many other points included. Choice C is then the obvious answer, and most directly relates to the closing sentences which it rewords.

Correcting Sentences

4. B

Sentence 4 is a fragment. "Not to mention resolving the conflicts between warring nations."

This sentence is essentially a verbal phrase of the word "resolve" which does not have a main clause as part of the sentence. It is the extension of the sentence preceding it which contains the main clause and does make sense as it stands after the sentence with the main clause. However, since it does not have the main clause in its own structure, it is a sentence fragment.

5. A
The following changes to sentence 6 would focus attention on the main idea in paragraph 2. "Yet, the technology behind the atom bomb essentially had the power of resolving the war itself which scientists like him failed to convey."

The use of the connector "No matter what" in the original sentence is irrelevant given the sense expressed in both the sentences it connects. Taking the context of paragraph into consideration, the use of the connector "Yet" complements the sense expressed in both the sentences.

6. B
Suggested changes for sentence 5, "For instance, the atom bomb was developed during the Second World War by the recommendations of the great Albert Einstein - who is accepted as the father of modern physics - in fear of the Germans developing it and using on the Allies."

The original sentence lacks a comma after the thought extension phrase "For instance." Also, the use of dash to link two or more ideas and make a point has been incomplete.

7. C
The following sentence, if inserted before sentence 7, would best illustrate the main idea of the passage, "Nuclear fission that is used in the fuelling of the bomb, has the capacity to produce electrical energy which has turned out to be a major alternative later in the Twentieth Century."

The main idea of the passage is the misuse of science regarding the development of the atom bomb during the Second World War, whereas it could effectively be used in meeting the energy demands of the countries involved in the war. This is expressed explicitly in the sentence offered in choice C, which is at the same time coherent with the seventh and eighth sentence between which it is being suggested to be placed. Other choices either lack coherence or are less relevant.

Practice Test Questions 2

8. A
Sentence 4 is a fragment. "Which I doubt belongs to any <u>other</u> person."

This sentence is an extension of the sentence preceding it. It does not complete the thought when alone, and is thus a sentence fragment.

9. A
Sentence 3 sentence is not consistent with the author's purpose. "For example, for an air stewardess position, girls have to be no more than 163 cm tall; whereas for jobs in foreign affairs, Chinese diplomats are required to match their foreign counterparts."

The passage talks about the people who want to increase their height by undergoing a surgery and points out the minimum height requirements for getting a job that they wish to work in. However, the expression "no more than 163 cm tall" is a statment about a maximum not a minimum. In addition, the sentence refers to Chinese diplomats who must 'match' the height of their foreign counterparts, which could be taller, and hence require surgery, or could be shorter and not require surgery.

10. B
The following sentence, if inserted after sentence 7, would best illustrate the main idea of the passage, "This artificial way of gaining height is turning out to be a new trend among the new generation in height conscious China."

The paragraph discusses about the application of leg surgery among Chinese young people to increase their height. This is best reflected in the sentence suggested in choice B which also contributes to the cohesion of the second paragraph as well as allowing a smooth transition between the second and third paragraph.

11. B
Suggested changes to sentence 8, "Even parents approve of the idea, being fully aware of all the complications and they are willing to finance such a sophisticated surgery."

The usage of vocabulary is incorrect in this sentence. The word "complexity" is an adjective noun used to describe detailed aspects of a given subject which is less relevant here. The word "labyrinth" is also incorrect in this context. The correct counterpart for "complexity" here, would be "complications" which takes into account the length of the surgery itself and the agony, sacrifice and the commitment associated with it, all in one. Also the word "sophisticated", as suggested in choices B and C in the place of "labyrinth" is more appropriate as it hints about the details of the surgery. Choice B offers both changes.

12. A
Sentence 4 is a fragment. "Which I doubt belongs to any other person."
This sentence is an extension of the sentence preceding it. It does not complete the thought when alone and is thus a sentence fragment.

13. D
Sentence 9 is the least relevant to the main idea of the second paragraph. "He is panicked by street dogs and neighbors' cats and to avoid them, he crosses to the other side of the street every now and then."

The second paragraph mainly talks about Luke's odd behavior while in a moving in a crowd, but sentence 9 shifts the subject to his strategy when he encounters cats and dog in the streets.

14. C
Sentence 4 contains a redundant phrase. "Which I doubt any other person belongs to other than him."

In this sentence the second "other" is redundant. It can be omitted.

15. B
The following sentence, if inserted before sentence 1, would best illustrate the main idea of the passage. "But that does not bother him; rather he always seems to be happy in being able to utter those two words."

Practice Test Questions 2

The passage starts with the speculation that Luke is probably the only person happy with his peculiar character and style of living. This is reflected in the sentence which is suggested to be added as the last sentence. Other choices do not offer the same relevance and coherence.

16. D
Sentence 6 is a fragment, "But for a day only."

This sentence fails to complete a thought when it stands alone. It is complementary as a thought extension to the previous sentence though and makes perfect sense when it is preceded by that. Since it neither has a noun clause, nor a verbal, it is a sentence fragment.

17. C
Sentence 8 is not consistent with author's purpose. "But as they came to know him closely, they were disappointed he would only occupy Mr. Drodsky's position for two weeks."

In sentence 6, the author indicates that the new teacher is replacing Mr. Drodsky for one day only. However, in sentence 8, it is clearly stated that he will be replacing him for two weeks, contradicting his earlier statement.

18. A
Suggested changes to sentence 16, "Coming from a public school in New Jersey, Ray had never seen students 'tamed' to such narrow, disparate discipline in his six years of experience as a music teacher."

The original sentence contains the wrong usage of the word "desperate." The use of the homophone "disparate" is more suited to express the distinct trait of the students in the new school he has joined. The right modification is suggested in choice A and all other choices offer incorrect changes.

19. D
Sentence 7 contains non-standard usage, "Aa you wiss me, chilsren?"

This sentence refers to Mr. Drodsky's Eastern European accent that can be considered as non-standard usage. Although strictly incorrect, it is permissible stylistically to illustrate his accent.

20. D
Sentence 5 is a fragment. "Hanging in between two sides of the wall near one corner of the store room which they rarely open, a magnificent piece of art left half woven and still being worked on."

This sentence does not express a complete thought since it does not have a verbal clause. A possible revision would be: "Hanging between two walls near one corner of the store room , lies a magnificent piece of art left half woven and still being worked on."

Vocabulary

1. B
Heinous: adj. shocking, terrible or wicked.

2. A
Harbinger: n. a person of thing that tells or announces the coming of someone or something

3. B
Judicious: Having, or characterized by, good judgment or sound thinking.

4. B
Ethanol: n. a colorless volatile flammable liquid C_2H_6O.

5. A
Respiratory: adj. Of, relating to, or affecting respiration or the organs of respiration.

6. B
Inherent: Naturally a part or consequence of something.

7. A
Vapid: adj. tasteless or bland.

Practice Test Questions 2

8. C
Waif: n. homeless child or stray.

9. D
Homologous: adj. similar or identical.

10. B
Obsolete: adj. no longer in use; gone into disuse; disused or neglected.

11. A
Rankle: v. To cause irritation or deep bitterness.

12. D
Reusable

13. C
Torpid: adj. Lazy, lethargic or apathetic.

14. A
Gregarious: adj. Describing one who enjoys being in crowds and socializing.

15. B
Mutation: n. a change or alteration.

16. C
Lithe: adj. flexible or pliant.

17. A
Resent: v. to express displeasure or indignation.

18. A
Immaterial: irrelevant not having substance or matter.

19. A
Impeccable: adj. perfect, no faults or errors.

20. B
Pudgy: adj. fat, plump or overweight.

English

1. C

The semicolon is used in a list where the list items have internal punctuation, such as "Key West, Florida."

2. C

The semicolon links independent clauses. An independent clause can form a complete sentence by itself.

3. A

The semicolon links independent clauses with a conjunction (However).

4. B

The sentence is correct. The semicolon links independent clauses. An independent clause can form a complete sentence by itself.

5. B

Double negative sentence. In double negative sentences, one negatives is replaced with "any."

6. A

The third conditional is used for talking about an unreal situation (that did not happen) in the past. For example, "If I had studied harder, [if clause] I would have passed the exam [main clause]. Which is the same as, "I failed the exam, because I didn't study hard enough."

7. D

Present perfect. You cannot use the Present Perfect with specific time expressions such as: yesterday, one year ago, last week, when I was a child, at that moment, that day, one day, etc. The Present Perfect is used with unspecific expressions such as: ever, never, once, many times, several times, before, so far, already, yet, etc.

8. C

Bring vs. Take. Usage depends on your location. Something coming your way is brought to you. Something going away is taken from you.

Practice Test Questions 2

9. A
The sentence is correct. Went vs. Gone. Went is the simple past tense. Gone is used in the past perfect.

10. B
Fewer vs. Less. 'Fewer' is used with countables and 'less' is used with uncountables.

11. D
Its vs. It's. 'It's' is a contraction for it is or it has. 'Its' is a possessive pronoun meaning, more or less, of 'it,' or belonging to 'it.'

12. D
When using 'however,' place a comma before and after.

13. B
"Who" is the best choice because the sentence refers to a person.

14. A
Past perfect is the correct form because it refers to something that happened in the past (he was the greatest inventor) and is still true today.

15. C
The superlative "hottest" is used when expressing the highest degree, or a degree greater than that of anything it is compared with.

16. D
When comparing two, use 'the taller.' When comparing more than two, use 'the tallest.'

17. B
Here the word "sale" is used as a "word" and not as a word in the sentence, so quotation marks are used.

18. C
His father is a poet and a novelist. It is necessary to use 'a' twice in this sentence for the two distinct things.

19. C
Titles of short stories are enclosed in quotation marks, and commas always go inside quotation marks.

20. B
Present tense, "ran well" is correct. "Ran good" is never correct.

21. D
Punctuation always goes inside quotation marks.

22. D
Healthful vs. Healthy. 'Healthy' is used to describe something that is of good for your health and 'healthful' refers to habits or types.

23. A
In vs. Into. 'In' a room means inside. 'Into' refers to movement or action.

24. C
Lay vs. Lie. Lie requires an object and lay does not. So you can lie down, (no object. and you lay a book on the floor.

25. A
The third conditional is used for talking about an unreal situation (that did not happen) in the past. For example, "If I had studied harder, [if clause] I would have passed the exam [main clause]. Which is the same as, "I failed the exam, because I didn't study hard enough."

26. A
Learn vs. Teach. Learning is what students do, and teaching is what teachers do.

27. B
Lose vs. Loose. Lose is to no longer have, or to lose a race. Loose is not tied or able to move freely.

28. D
Persecute vs. Prosecute. To prosecute is to have a legal claim against someone and to persecute is to harass.

Practice Test Questions 2

29. A
Precede vs. Proceed. To precede is to go first or in front of. To proceed is to go forward.

30. A
Quoted speech is not capitalized.

31. A
The sentence is correct. Periods and events are capitalized but not century numbers.

32. C
Brand names are capitalized.

33. B
Generic terms such as 'french fries' are not capitalized. Brand names are capitalized.

34. C
The names of sports teams, as proper nouns, are capitalized. In this sentence, the full name is capitalized, Blue Jays.

35. A
The sentence is correct. North, South, East, and West when used as sections of the country, but not as compass directions.

Conclusion

Congratulations! You have made it this far because you have applied yourself diligently to practicing for the exam and no doubt improved your potential score considerably! Getting into a good school is a huge step in a journey that might be challenging at times but will be many times more rewarding and fulfilling. That is why being prepared is so important.

Study then Practice and then Succeed!

Good Luck!

Register for Free Updates and More Practice Test Questions

Register your purchase at
https://www.test-preparation.ca/register/
for updates, free test tips and more practice test questions.

https://www.facebook.com/CompleteTestPreparation/

https://www.youtube.com/user/MrTestPreparation

ONLINE RESOURCES

How to Prepare for a Test - The Ultimate Guide

https://www.test-preparation.ca/prepare-test/

Learning Styles - The Complete Guide

https://www.test-preparation.ca/learning-style/

Test Anxiety Secrets!

https://www.test-preparation.ca/test-anxiety/

Time Management on a Test

https://www.test-preparation.ca/time-management/

Flash Cards - The Complete Guide

https://www.test-preparation.ca/flash-cards/

Test Preparation Video Series

https://www.test-preparation.ca/test-video/

How to Memorize - The Complete Guide

https://www.test-preparation.ca/memorize/

Online Library of Student Tips and Strategies

https://www.test-preparation.ca/students-say/

Visit us Online

WWW.TEST-PREPARATION.CA